This book is the first project from <u>The Rebel Within Us</u>
a new venture from Jason SurfrApp

Learn more about how to unleash your inner creativity
and find your inner rebel at
www.therebelwithinus.com

BRAD,
your FRIEND ERIC PALMER
WANTED TO SURPRISE you WITH
THIS COPY OF MY NEW BOOK!!
I HOPE you ENJOY IT!

(THE AUTHOR)

This book was written by Jason SurfrApp
This book was edited and formatted by Round Table Companies
The book cover and illustrations were done by Caroline Winegeart

978-0-692-20794-9, ISBN

This book was made possible by over 300 sponsors and supporters.
Without them, Creativity For Sale would never have happened.
Feel free to take content from this book and share/replicate it, but
please link back *CreativityForSale.com*. Sharing is caring!

Printed in Canada

CREATIVITY FOR SALE

HOW I MADE 1,000,000 WEARING T-SHIRTS AND HOW
YOU CAN TURN YOUR PASSION INTO PROFIT, TOO

TABLE OF CONTENTS

ON THE BOTTOM OF
EACH PAGE OF THIS BOOK
YOU'LL FIND A FUN
SPONSORED MESSAGE

INTRODUCTION: JASON _____ ?

For the past 32 years of my life, only one thing has been consistent: change. I wasn't a military brat, but growing up, I lived in Arizona, California, Virginia, New Jersey, and eventually Florida. My mom and I still argue about the correct number, but I attended somewhere between 12 and 16 schools. Not only did I attend double the amount of schools that normal kids do, but when I changed schools, it was often to a new city or a different state. I was the "new kid" over and over again.

Let it be known that I don't hold a grudge against my mom for this, and I wouldn't change my upbringing one bit because it made me who I am today. Okay, maybe I'd change asking Yolanda to middle school prom. When I found her phone number in the school phone book, I called her and asked her to go with me, and she said promptly said no and hung up. But that's a story for another book.

Being the new kid over and over felt like living in that MC Escher painting with all the staircases. Just when I thought I had navigated the right direction, made a few friends, and gotten into a rhythm, we moved. Three of those moves happened in high school, which were the hardest on me. Imagine yourself back in high school, but instead of the high school you went to and knew well, imagine a different high school. In this high school, you don't know where anything is (except maybe the principal's office), and you don't know a single person. Walking through the halls and going to class isn't too difficult, but you have the constant feeling that everyone is staring at you because you're the new kid, the new face, and you stick out like a sore thumb.

But lunch, oh man, lunch. Walking through the cafeteria doors and looking at all the other students who already have friends and tables to sit at is the worst. As you scan the lunchroom, it becomes painfully obvious that you don't know where to sit, but you also don't want to wait too long to find a seat or you'll look like the creepy kid holding his lunch and standing in the cafeteria doorway by himself. There's an open table or two, and once you find a seat at one of them, you can't get to it fast enough. It doesn't sound like a whole lot of fun, right? Like I said, it wasn't easy.

When you eat your lunch by yourself, you are truly alone with your teenage angst. At some high schools, I ate lunch by myself for only a day or two before a kind stranger came up to say hello or I found another misfit sitting alone to talk to. At other high schools, though, I went weeks eating alone or I avoided the cafeteria altogether.

But don't cry for me, Argentina! Looking back, these experiences helped mold me into the entrepreneur I would become. Those painful times I spent alone helped me become more extroverted throughout the rest of my life. I didn't want to experience the pain of sitting alone or feeling like I didn't have any friends. Thinking about those tough times helps me walk up to a complete stranger nowadays and say hello. Sure, I may have spent many an hour sitting alone in cafeterias, but that thickened my skin up for the brief few moments before that awkward hello when you meet a new person (which really only sucks for a few seconds). I learned how to adapt to change and how to make the best of any situation—two lessons that would come in handy as I started my businesses.

During all the time of movement, I also had multiple fathers come in and out of my life. Having multiple father figures brought me some good experiences and some not-so-good experiences, but overall it taught me that I was capable of taking care of myself. I developed a sense of independence because of it, and I think that independence translated itself into my out-of-the-box thinking later in life.

I also had a myriad of retail and customer service jobs when I was younger that taught me about identifying value, building human connections with different types of people, and prioritizing my money. I interned at a large insurance company in New York City as a graphic designer, commuting via train from New Jersey to the city daily with my buddy Alun Evans (page 24's sponsor, by the way). I learned how to deal with multiple bosses, how to manage important project deadlines, and that I really didn't like wearing a suit to work. I had another graphic design gig, but this time for an online coffee startup during the dotcom boom. I cared nothing about coffee when I worked for that company, but I made sure to suck it up and get the work done. I learned the important art of Photoshopping clear plastic on different color backgrounds (a skill everyone needs!). This was also the first, and only, job I was ever "downsized" from. I learned that I never wanted to feel that pain again, especially when I had worked hard for a company I didn't even have any interest in.

The first "real" job I had out of college was actually a dream job on paper. I worked for the ATP (Association of Tennis Professionals) as a graphic designer. The idea of working for a large sports agency was glamorous to me because I was (and am) a huge fan of the NFL and NBA. What started as an incredibly positive work experience quickly showed me that I wasn't cut out for the 9–5 world. Things like climbing the corporate ladder, attending meaningless meetings, working with unhappy people, and feeling like I never saw results (monetarily or job growth-wise) taught me some valuable lessons about what I **didn't** want to do for a living. And all of this work experience was before I ever considered myself an entrepreneur. Yet, looking back, each one taught me things about myself, about business, and mostly about the fact that I didn't really enjoy working for other people.

Toward the end of my three and a half year career at the ATP, I had been chatting with a fellow design friend, Dennis Eusebio, about starting our own design company. I just knew that something inside me would never be happy unless I was my own boss. We decided to take the plunge, and we founded what became my first company, Thought & Theory. For the better part of six months, I worked at the ATP from 9–5 days, and I worked at Thought & Theory from 7:00 p.m. to midnight. Dennis and I agreed that I would transition away from doing design work and focus on the client management, marketing, and sales skills I had honed over the years.

During the first year and a half of operation, many of the Thought & Theory clients asked me about social media—if they should be doing something with Twitter, Facebook, and YouTube. We hadn't used those sites, so I didn't know how to answer. But client after client mentioned these sites, and with each call or email, I got more interested in learning about them. I had *heard* of Facebook and Twitter, and had watched my weight in silly cat videos on YouTube, but I didn't see these mediums as valuable to me. (My, how things change.)

Eventually, I poked around on social networks enough to notice that businesses were on them, but that they weren't doing much. There were millions of people already on these networks, but no way for businesses to connect directly with them. I knew that there were spokespeople for brands and companies on TV, radio, billboards, etc., but there seemed to be nothing like that on social media, and I made a mental note.

Then one morning I found myself standing in my closet trying to figure out what t-shirt I would wear from the dozens that I owned. That's when the light bulb went on. Almost every company in the world could make t-shirts to promote its business . . . so what if *I* wore a company's t-shirt and shared that through these free social media websites?

That day was September 24, 2008, and that's when the seed for IWearYourShirt was officially planted.

Throughout this book, I'll share with you how IWearYourShirt went from an idea I had in my closet to a business that generated over $1,000,000 in revenue. IWearYourShirt taught me that creativity is the key component to developing a business and lifestyle that you love. It taught me that anything is truly possible if you have an imagination and if you're willing to put in the necessary work. (I mean, if you're going to trust somebody that says, "Anything is possible," I say trust the guy who made a sizable living by simply getting dressed in the morning.)

I'll also pull back the curtain on my business a bit and share all my successes and failures along the way. My previous work experiences in life may have helped me develop some client management, marketing, and sales skills, but most of what I learned was through trial and error (. . . and mostly error!). My hope is that you'll not only learn from my mistakes, but that you'll also see that creating a successful business isn't some unattainable thing. You don't have to have it all figured out from the beginning. You just need an idea or a talent that you're passionate about and the courage to learn as you go.

youtube.com/michaelgebben - A YouTube channel helps people have light-bulb moments! Those moments when you realize ANYTHING is possible!

Later on in the book, I'll go into detail on how to think outside the box for your next idea or business. I'll also explain how my unconventional thinking has been one of my strongest assets over the years, and I'll lead you through the entire process of setting the foundation to make money doing what you love. Whether you're stuck or unmotivated or just plain lost, hopefully this book will be the spark you need to go after your dreams.

I set out to write an unconventional book because everything I do in business is pretty unconventional. If you take away just one thing from it all, I want you to remember that I'm no one special. I'm just a guy who likes to think outside the box. I refuse to let my life be dictated by others, and I hope you'll join me in that after reading this book. Do work that matters to you, and don't be afraid to do things wildly differently from other people. In fact, please share whatever awesome thing you are doing with me via email. I'd love to hear about it: *jason@sponsormybook.com. (After you finish the book, obviously.)*

Now let's get those creative juices flowing!

SECTION 1:
JASON

When I told people I thought I could get companies to pay me to wear their t-shirts, more than a few people called me crazy. In this section, I take you through what it was like to take that "crazy" idea and grow it into a thriving, reputable business.

Chapter 1

LET ME WEAR YOUR SHIRT

On the morning of October 10, 2008, I sat on my couch with my dog, Plaxico, and stared at my laptop in utter confusion. Overnight, my design and development team had finished putting the final touches on the IWearYourShirt website. It wasn't an extravagant website, but it was the first big project I'd ever undertaken solo, and a large photo of me was plastered on the front page of it. I had seen previous iterations of the website, but pieces of it were all over the place before that morning. Now, it was a completed object. All the puzzle pieces finally fit together, and it was ready for the world to see it. There was just one problem. When launch time came, instead of seeing a fiery blaze of sales and hockey stick shaped web traffic, all I heard was my dog snoring and the morning weather report from my TV.

I had spent the previous evening clicking around every square inch of IWearYourShirt.com. I wasn't hoping to find hidden Internet gold—no no. I wanted to make sure everything was perfect. On a normal day, I followed a typical routine: wake up, make breakfast, let the dog out, use the restroom, and maybe even shower. Not

Badger.com - The domain registrar Jason used for Creativity For Sale. Badger is domain management you'll enjoy! Check us out!

today. Today I went from horizontal in my bed to hunched over my laptop on my couch in a hurry. My bowels and Plaxico could wait.

As the day progressed, my morning excitement turned to late evening sombertude. IWearYourShirt was the greatest idea I had ever had. It was going to be a new way for businesses to advertise. I was going to make a bunch of money and become famous, right? Yet, do you know how many people visited the website on that day? Twelve. Ten of those people were probably the designer and the developer doing updates, and then another was me refreshing the website incessantly. The other two were probably from my mom and grandmother. That was all it was. Nobody purchased a single day on the IWearYourShirt calendar (*hold your horses, explanation of this coming!*). Mike Tyson has never punched me in the gut, but that morning, I imagined I knew what it felt like.

When the clock ticked past 2:00 a.m. that same day, I finally threw in the towel with a heavy heart and a bruised ego and closed my laptop. I laid in bed for hours, wide awake, like a mummy-zombie. I didn't toss and turn. I didn't look at my phone. I just laid flat on my back and stared at the ceiling, wondering why this amazing project hadn't become wildly successful on launch day. Eventually, my mind and body shut down and I fell asleep. As I drifted off, a part of me still had a glimmer of hope that I'd wake up to a slew of emails, calendar purchases, and praise from all corners the world.

Remember when I told you to hold your horses? You can let them go! Let me back up for a second for those of you who may not be familiar with IWearYourShirt (IWYS). The basic idea for the business was that each day I would wear a business's t-shirt, take a photo, film a video, and promote that business and the content I created on different social media sites. The calendar that I mentioned was how I sold my t-shirt advertising space. As of that morning on

October 10, 2008, every day in 2009 was for sale. The price would start at $1 on January 1. On January 2, the price would increase to $2. On January 3, the price would increase to $3. The price increased by $1 per day until December 31, which went for $365.

The original pricing structure I had thought of was a flat fee of $100 per day. However, the math showed me that the $1-per-day pricing would net $66,795 and the $100 flat-fee pricing would only net $36,500. (I'd like to point out 365 × 100 is easy math. Figuring out the $1-per-day total involved creating an Excel spreadsheet and filling out 365 individual cells with 1, 2, 3, 4, 5 . . . up to 365. Then I Googled how to add up a bunch of cells in Excel. I've since learned simple summation in Excel.) I wasn't a math whiz, but I knew 66 was more than 36. I also knew that I couldn't charge much in the beginning because no one had ever heard of IWYS or me. Over time, I would grow a larger following online, warranting a higher price to be spent later in the year. I'd also like to point out that my time spent on the pricing model was about one hour. The majority of that hour (98.5% of it) was the aforementioned Excel spreadsheet.

The morning after launch day began with the same disappointment in which the previous day ended. I didn't even bother getting out of bed; I grabbed my iPhone off my nightstand and checked my email and website traffic. Nothing. It was around 9:00 a.m., and there was no chance I'd be able to fall back asleep. I decided to avoid heading to work (my couch) right away and hopped in the shower. It was during those steam-and-soap-filled 10 minutes that I thought, "How could I have such a unique and different idea, with no one coming to buy?" I was feeling the mixture of confusion at why my brilliance hadn't been received, trying to brainstorm what had gone wrong, and being bummed out about the whole thing.

Then it hit me like a bolt of shower-lightning. I had no existing network and hadn't shared the IWYS website with anyone. The personal Facebook account I had was actually set up by my college roommate, Travis, and I didn't have loads of friends. I had a personal Twitter account, but it didn't have more than 30 followers at the time. The IWYS Twitter account had even fewer.

Hell, I hadn't even emailed my existing contacts when the site launched.

Then shower-lightning struck again: How in the world will anyone know I started this company and launched this website if I don't tell them?

By the time I was done in the shower, my thoughts went from lost and sad to hopeful and encouraged. With a towel wrapped around my waist, I made a beeline for the couch and flipped open my laptop. It was time to put my nose to the grindstone. To start, I emailed all of the contacts I could scrounge up from my three different email addresses (one of which was an AOL email, #lol). I didn't want to ask all of these people to buy days on IWYS; I just wanted them to know the project existed.

I also wanted to hear back from as many of them as I could, so I sent individual emails to each person instead of one bulk message with a simple question at the end: *What do you think of IWear-YourShirt, and will you pass this along to any friends who might be interested in it?*

I had never done email marketing before in my life, but I knew the value of email, and I appreciated someone taking the time to send me a personalized note.

Three hours later, I finished emailing my 200 contacts. Still in my towel, which was now completely dry, I felt motivated. I even started seeing some email replies come in while I was writing and sending others. I also received a text message from the website developer that there was a spike in web traffic. I think it was something like "5 visitors to 30 visitors," but hey, that's a traffic increase of 600%! As I started to read the email replies, I noticed a trend. One reply would be positive, with a message of encouragement and excitement for me. The next would say something like, "This idea is stupid . . . don't quit your day job." Reading those emails was an emotional rollercoaster, especially because the majority of these 200 email contacts were friends and family. But I noticed something. There were more positive responses than negative ones. And the negative responses actually added fuel to my encouragement fire. The more negative emails I read, the more I wanted to prove those people wrong. I knew what it was like to feel different from my days back in high school, searching for a table to sit at in the cafeteria. Through all those years we moved around, eventually I stopped caring what people thought about me. That lesson is what helped me push through those early days when people said I was crazy, and it's a lesson that helps me continue to push the envelope with every business or project I start.

Chapter 2

LET THERE
BE SALES!

At some point during the email melee, I took a break. I let my dog out, put on clothes, and smeared gobs of peanut butter on two slices of multigrain bread. Between and during each task, I refreshed my email inbox on my iPhone like a crazy person. I'm shocked I didn't spread peanut butter on my dog's head and end up wearing socks on my arms because I was so distracted.

Then a magical thing happened . . . the first calendar purchase came in. This was my moment. This was it.

Then I read who purchased it: Thought & Theory.

Dang it, Dennis! Dennis was the co-founder of my design company, Thought & Theory, where I was still working "full-time," expecting IWearYourShirt to only amount to a side gig. I sent him a text message thanking him for the whopping $4 that had just been sent to my bank account.

A few minutes later, another purchase came in. This time it was from one of our clients, Benjamin Edgar. January 3 was officially sold (mind you, it was for $3). This was the first outside person to buy a day, and it was all because I sent him an email sharing IWYS.

Get the exact system that helped more than 40 entrepreneurs raise over $4 million on Kickstarter and Indiegogo at www.crowdfundinghacks.com/jason

I actually still have the email he sent me after making the purchase. If you're reading this, Ben, thanks for being the first official day purchaser of IWYS (not sure I ever told him that).

By the end of the day, 50 people had responded to my emails. Thirty of those emails were positive and encouraging; the rest were people who were Negative Neds/Nancys.

With only two purchases, it surely wasn't the tsunami of sharing and buying I had hoped for, but it was a step in the right direction. I wouldn't say I was on cloud nine, but I was definitely feeling better than the night before. I spent the remainder of the day at my favorite taco place (see TacoLu on page 69), celebrating over a few margaritas and chips and salsa. The dinner probably cost me $50, and I had only made $7 that day. But hey, the margaritas were delicious!

The only company from Fargo, ND in this book? Myriad Mobile. We know, you're thinking, "Like the movie?" You bet. Learn more on page 140.

Chapter 3

ONE HUNDRED FORTY CHARACTERS

The next morning, my email inbox could have been the dust bowl of Oklahoma during the Great Depression, minus the tumbleweeds. Shrugging it off, I figured I had done all I could with email, so I shifted my focus to Twitter. There, I searched for anyone talking about advertising, t-shirts, and marketing. I spent the better part of that third day tweeting at complete strangers from the IWYS Twitter account. I sent witty and funny tweets. I sent silly photos of me in t-shirts, and I argued with a few people about font treatments (I don't care about font treatments at all; I just wanted conversation).

In the back of my mind, I was hoping my Twitter handle alone would pique some interest and bring in sales. It did bring interest, but mostly in people following me, not in sales. It wasn't the perfect ROI I'd hoped for, but I knew having more followers would be good in general. I felt way less enthusiastic about my immediate results with Twitter, but I received much less negative feedback (which was a plus).

During the time I transitioned away from email and was scouring Twitter for keywords and talking to random people around the world, another email hit my inbox from Chris Yeh. Chris mentioned he had an introduction for me. Chris was one of the first complete strangers to find my IWYS Twitter account and @ mention me, long before I ever launched. A few weeks earlier, he had sent an email saying he admired my creativity and thought IWYS was a great idea (I have no clue how he found my IWYS Twitter account, but Twitter was a much smaller place back then so maybe he was searching keywords as well?). After reading Chris' email, I did what any curious person does: I Googled him. Chris was an entrepreneur, advisor, and an investor. We chatted a few times on the phone before IWYS launched, and it was always incredibly enlightening to chat with him. We talked about thinking big picture for IWYS, and he helped spur the $1-per-day pricing model idea.

Chris suggested I connect with a young public relations (PR) guy by the name of Evan White who was doing work for one of the companies in which Chris was an investor, Ustream.tv. I had heard of Ustream.tv when I was doing initial research on YouTube and other video platforms, and I knew that their goal was to be the online source for *live* video content . . . but that was as much as I knew. Naturally, Google pointed me to a simple website with a video featuring Evan. In it, Evan sat poolside, his blackberry in hand, flip-flops on his feet, wearing sunglasses and a slightly cocked hat. From the video, I could tell he was a fun guy, and his personality resonated with me. (This was actually my first introduction to a PR person. As it turns out they all don't wear flip-flops and sit poolside.)

After a few emails, Evan and I jumped on a phone call. He talked about some of his previous PR work and about living near the beach in California. I talked about some of my previous design work and about living near the beach in Florida. We ended up having a ton in common, and he was interested in helping IWYS get some media

· 17 ·

Go to page 115.

attention. I also think he said the word "cool" or "awesome" more times than I did, which was rare in another human being.

A day or two later, Evan called and said he had convinced Ustream.tv to buy January 1 for $1. In return for having Day 1, they wanted me to host my own Ustream show each day in my branded t-shirt, and they would promote my show on their homepage. At the time, the viewership of Ustream.tv wasn't high, but whatever it was would bring in more than my existing 30 website visits, *that was for sure*. I was nervous to accept the $1 offer, but I knew if I had planned on learning how to film a YouTube video each day, I could figure out how to host a live video show each day, so I pulled the trigger and agreed. Shortly thereafter, $1 showed up in the IWYS PayPal account (which ended up actually being $0.98 after fees). And so began an era that would lead to 889 consecutive days of sharing my daily shirt-wearing antics and my life on a live video stream for the world to see, every single day from 3–4:00 p.m. ET, like clockwork.

Chapter 4

USTREAM . . . ?

On December 8, 2008, I hosted my first Ustream.tv live show that was promoted on the Ustream.tv homepage. This show was a pre-launch show of sorts—an attempt to build a little buzz and excitement, before I really knew what those things were. (Remember, official shirt-wearing wasn't set to begin until January 1, 2009.) I had done a few test shows before that to make sure my laptop camera worked and to find a backdrop that looked better than my brown couch and beige wall, but not a single viewer tuned in to witness that.

When I went live on December 8, my laptop sat atop the TV in my bedroom, and Ustream put my show on their homepage. The viewers started to come in. Then they started to pour in. Thanks to Ustream's viewer count on my screen, I knew exactly how many people were watching at a given time. I was a nervous wreck at first, trying to fill dead air time, find things to talk about, and mask how sweaty I actually was. I talked about everything from my dog Plaxico, to living in Florida, to what I ate that day, to what IWYS was all about, and some other gobbledygook.

After two hours, over 8,000 people had tuned in to watch my first Ustream show. Many viewers stayed the entire time, including

MEMOJI.com is an online marketplace that curates purposeful, aesthetic, and creative workspace tools to inspire passionate professionals.

one Stacy Lunsford (aka Digimap) who still supports IWYS and me to this day. You rock, Digi!

When that show was over, I felt fantastic. My adrenaline was pumping. My shirt was soaked in sweat, and I had gained a couple hundred new Twitter followers. A handful of people emailed me to say IWYS was "brilliant." And three days sold on the calendar. Not bad for my first show.

Looking back, tapping into the Ustream audience was one of the biggest accelerators for IWearYourShirt's growth. Not only did it allow me to leverage an existing network (something that was still virtually non-existent for me at the time), but it also allowed me to connect with people on a daily basis. I viewed my show not just as a one-way vehicle for entertainment but as a two-way vehicle for engagement. People would stop by to watch and chat with me in Ustream's text chat box. I made it a point to learn about those people and to really care about who they were. Many of those early viewers went on to become long-term fans of the brand; they were critical because I needed to show sponsors that people were interested in consuming their branded content.

Chapter 5

(()LEVERAGE

A few days after my first Ustream show, Evan emailed to say that a *New York Times* reporter wanted to do a story on IWYS. I'm not sure how Evan had talked this reporter into writing a story about IWYS, but I'm assuming he used some secret PR-ninja tactics. I had never imagined the *NYTimes* would be my first big media hit.

I received an email from Jenna Wortham, and it was direct and to the point.

"Evan White referred me to you—I'd like to know more about your experiment. Have a sec to chat today, either on AIM or Gchat?"

That was it.

What happened to email foreplay right? I responded with my Gchat name, and we started chatting right then. With each question she asked, I'm fairly certain I gave an answer that was way too long and full of grammatical errors. During the long breaks between questions (read: impatient seconds due to my excitement), I (naturally) Googled Jenna. (Come on, we all do it.)

Her photo was one of the first results. She had a stylish poof of black hair, wore large, black-rimmed hipster glasses, and had on bright red lipstick. I skimmed a few of her articles while answering her questions, and my excitement built like a volcano. I remember

Tired of your unruly phone chargers? Check out what Chargertamer can do for you: www.chargertamer.com

wanting to type over and over again: "HOLY &$^#! I'M GOING TO BE IN *THE NEW YORK TIMES*!" But of course, I played it cool.

What seemed like a conversation that lasted hours (mostly due to the wait time between my answers and her next question) was over in mere minutes. The entire IWYS story up to that point, which frankly wasn't much, had been sent through a tiny rectangle on a window in Gmail. When the conversation was over and I closed the chat window, I thought this was "it." *This* was the moment. IWYS was going to be everywhere!

BEING FEATURED IN THE MEDIA OFFERS YOU OPPORTUNITY BEYOND THE STORY ITSELF.

Then the funniest thing happened. Jenna said the story wouldn't run for another month. I was devastated. Surely the *NYTimes* wanted to run my story immediately, right? Wasn't it unbelievably creative and unique? Wasn't it breaking news for *NYTimes*? I called Evan to have him join me while I drowned in my sorrows.

Immediately, Evan's PR experience kicked into high gear. He told me we didn't need the actual story itself to be up, we just needed the commitment so we could use it as leverage. The eventual *NYTimes* article became a piece of bait that we dangled in front of anyone and everyone we could. Evan told me he'd send emails to his contacts and that I should email all of my contacts again with the news that the *NYTimes* had "interviewed me for a story."

Wait.

Why would anyone care if the interview wasn't actually up? Here's the first big lesson I learned about getting mentioned by the media: It creates a cloak of credibility. The *NYTimes* could have been writing an article that exposed stories about crazy people living in Florida. But I *was* going to be in that article. And I *was* interviewed by the *NYTimes*. The key was all in the messaging and how we positioned it to our contacts. I knew the story wasn't about crazy people in Florida, but I had never used media for leverage before, so this felt completely foreign to me. (The next time you see an "As featured in XYZ TV show" on someone's website, you'll probably be surprised to find what that feature was actually about and whether it was 100% dedicated to how amazing that person was.)

Over the next few days, I emailed all my contacts, which consisted of my original 200 and another 100 or so that had come in from Ustream, Twitter, and other random emails. I shared with them that I had just done an exciting interview with the *NYTimes* featuring IWearYourShirt and that it was to be going live soon on NYTimes.com. All of these things were 100% true. The interview was extremely exciting *for me*. I had been interviewed by someone at the *NYTimes*. The story they were doing would feature IWYS. And the story would exist somewhere on the NYTimes.com domain *soon* (though I had no clue where or precisely when).

It worked. And well. Soon people were sending email replies with their own excitement for me. People I had emailed originally that didn't email me back were now asking loads of questions about IWYS. Sales were coming in, too, faster than I could count. Over those few days, nearly 100 days sold on the IWYS calendar, and I barely knew anyone who purchased a day. I couldn't stop grinning from ear to ear. And I had effectively learned about leveraging media.

That early gain in momentum *did* have something to do with the *NYTimes* but not in the way that most people expect. It was the idea of being mentioned that was used effectively to gain traction and sales.

If there's one thing I've learned over the years from being featured on countless media outlets around the world, it's that the media coverage itself may not do much for you. However, the credibility it can provide is always valuable. When the *NYTimes* interview finally ran in February of 2009, I noticed almost no spike in web traffic and maybe one or two sales. It's how I *used* the credibility of being featured in the *NYTimes* that actually made the huge impact—not the article itself.

Oi! I'm Alun Evans & I am Jason's oldest friend. I'm a Real Estate agent in Oakville, Ont More about me at AlunEvans.com. You won't do it.

Chapter 6

CHRISTMAS HARO EVE

During my crash course in PR early on, Evan also email-introduced me to a gentleman named Peter Shankman from Help A Reporter Out (HARO). This email introduction came with a price, though, and Peter wasn't cheap. You see, Peter had created a huge email list of journalists and sources (in late 2008, approximately 50,000 people were on the list). Journalists would post requests for information and other subscribers of the email would answer those requests. It was a brilliant PR tool, and Peter had placed small text advertisements at the top of the email. I had never considered myself a salesman in the beginning stages of IWYS, but Peter Shankman—*he* was a salesman, and a damn good one at that.

Upon asking for the rates for the text advertisements at HARO, Peter waved success stories from other advertisers in my e-face, saying things like "So-and-so-company gained over 1,000 new customers!" and "John Doe's business was found by *USA Today.*" He had quotes from happy customers. Lots of fancy media outlet mentions. To Peter's credit, these things were all 100% true, and the advertising spots worked very well. And then I got to the bottom of his email and saw the price: $1,500.

At that time, even by selling nearly 100 days on the IWYS calendar, I had barely made $1,500 (selling out January, February, and March netted just over $2,000). Then came the real kicker. Peter mentioned that the ads were selling so well that the next available spot was in February (two months away!). I can remember forwarding Peter's email to Evan and saying simply ". . .".

I was just that: speechless. How could I afford to spend $1,500 with no clue that anyone would actually buy IWYS days? And, what if Peter was exaggerating or just sharing success stories that were few and far between? But Evan wasn't going to let my doubt get in the way. He believed HARO would work and told me if it didn't at least make the $1,500 back, he would pay the difference. That was an offer I couldn't refuse. Resolute, I emailed Peter back and booked the ad spot.

Over the next few days, I was like a kid on Christmas (Two Months Long) Eve. With each passing day came more and more impatience. Eventually, Peter sent me an unexpected email.

"Tomorrow's [Dec 22] afternoon spot just opened up. Do you want it?" Faster than you can say *Peter* I had responded "YESSS!" Then the Christmas Eve excitement went into *intense* overdrive. Not only was it *three days from actual Christmas Eve*, now it was Christmas HARO Eve as well. The 12-year-old me would have bounced off the walls like a lunatic. Instead, I handled the excitement like the adult that I am, drinking copious amounts of alcohol and eating my weight in pepperoni pizza. I know it may seem odd that I was this stoked for an ad spot, but in the back of my mind, I knew I needed something to help IWYS take off and hoped this was it.

By the time the ad was supposed to run, I had begun sweating bullets. This was a huge gamble, but instead of trying to hit 21 at a

Knock knock.

blackjack table in Vegas, I was trying to sell days on a virtual calendar of me wearing t-shirts.

The ad ran and the immediate spike in traffic was incredible. Over 3,000 unique visitors came through IWearYourShirt.com in a matter of an hour. And the sales. Oh, the sales! Over 50 people purchased days, bringing in over $8,000 in revenue in less than two hours. I had also landed a handful of new media contacts and interviews. If the Cookie Monster woke up to find his pillow, his sheets, the walls of his house, even his grass, to be made of warm, gooey chocolate chip cookies . . . this would most accurately portray the excitement that ripped through me that evening.

After the HARO smoke cleared and Christmas was over, I felt the mounting momentum as January 1, 2009—the official IWYS launch day—approached. By that time, the IWYS calendar was about 50% sold out, and I hadn't even started wearing the t-shirts yet. I attended a New Year's Eve party wearing my first t-shirt under my sport coat and button-up shirt. I enjoyed my time out with my friends, drank a little extra champagne, and made sure my friends took a couple photos of me enjoying the evening. Then, at 12:01 a.m., I ripped open my button-up shirt like Clark Kent to reveal the first sponsored shirt I would ever wear: Ustream.tv.

Several glasses of champagne later, I stumbled into my house, opened my laptop, and uploaded my first official shirt-wearing photos to IWearYourShirt.com. I published a pre-written hello message on the website, closed my laptop, sent Evan a text message that read something like "And it begins . . ." and went to sleep happy.

Who's there?

Chapter 7

MY FIRST DAY OF (T-SHIRT WEARING) SCHOOL

The next morning, on January 1, 2009, Google Analytics for IWearYourShirt.com revealed over 1,500 people had already been to the website. I was grinning ear to ear. It felt like my birthday and winning first place in a pancake-eating contest (with a trophy, obviously) all wrapped in to one. For months, I had spent countless hours sending emails and planning for this day. It had finally arrived, and seeing a spike in traffic was just the beginning. There were a few calendar purchases waiting for me in my inbox, as well as a few people waiting to buy who had questions. After answering those few important emails, it was time to document my new t-shirt wearing life. I drove to Chick-fil-A with my Flip video camera suction-cupped to the dashboard. I hit the record button and filmed myself driving and talking about Ustream while heading to breakfast. If this was how every day of my life would feel as a "professional t-shirt wearer," I was pretty damn pumped!

Oink. Oink.

Throughout the rest of the day, I answered questions through email and Twitter, posted photos on Facebook, and got ready for my first official live video show on Ustream. When the show went live at 3:00 p.m. EST, Ustream put it on the homepage of their site, as promised, and over 20,000 people watched. Most of that live show was a blur, but I went 90 minutes over my planned one-hour timeslot, and I felt like I had found my niche.

All the emotional ups and downs, all the "what ifs" that occurred the few months prior, were long gone. This was what I had hoped for on October 10 when I launched and nothing happened; it just took two and half months longer to achieve the feeling of success I had dreamed of. I imagine this is what NASA feels like when they shoot a rocket ship into space . . . Very similar to IWYS, I know.

After that first day, I could feel the momentum and it was incredible. Not only did it feel like months of hard work were finally paying off, but it also felt like my idea was a hit. It felt like I was providing value by doing something that was uniquely suited to me. The real work had just begun, of course, but I'll never forget that feeling. It's a feeling I hope everyone gets the chance to experience at least once: the feeling of creating something completely different and completely your own.

Oink oink who?

Chapter 8

LIFE-CHANGING EMAILS

In August 2009, I received an email from a small business columnist at Reuters who asked if I'd be interested in a five-day, "day in the life" interview article for them. Because he was booked with other stories for several months, we targeted the second week in November 2009, when I happened to be going on a 5-day t-shirt sponsored cruise by MSC Cruises (the MSC standing for Mediterranean Shipping Company). He was already excited to have me journal my life, but with a Caribbean cruise thrown in the mix, he was even happier.

In hindsight, that definitely seems glamorous. Getting paid to wear t-shirts for a living while going on an all-expenses-paid five-day cruise to the Caribbean. Not a bad gig. As the months went by, I had almost forgotten about my Reuters piece, until the same Reuters reporter reached out to me in early October. One of his producers had caught wind of my story and wanted to do an additional feature on me. He wanted to know if they could send a crew to my home in Jacksonville, Florida, to do the story in early November, but when I declined due to a previously booked a trip to New York City to attend a conference, his ears perked up. The Reuters headquarters

Make up your mind, are you a pig or an owl!?

was in Times Square, and filming a segment *there* would be even better. Win-win.

In early morning on November 4, 2009, I landed at the LaGuardia Airport, hopped in a cab, and headed to my hotel. Like a little kid, I sat with luggage on my lap the entire hour-long cab ride from the airport to my hotel. I'd been grinning from ear to ear since waking up, and it hadn't faded yet.

I checked in, dropped off my bags, and left my hotel to walk to the Thompson Reuters office in Times Square. I all but skipped from the hotel door to the Reuters office, brimming with excitement. I knew that Reuters handled big news. Global news. This story was going to be *huge* for IWYS. When I got to the Reuters building, I stood outside and stared up at their logo on the building. If a pickpocket was nearby, he could have taken my pants and shoes, and I wouldn't have even noticed or cared (just don't take my t-shirts!).

Inside at the reception area, a nice man in a button-up shirt and starched jeans greeted me with his cameraman counterpart.

"T-Shirt Guy!" he hollered in my direction.

We shook hands, made quick small talk, and walked outside to film the story. He told me he wanted to see me in my "t-shirt wearing element," so I pulled out my Flip video camera and started to film my daily video. I finished my video filming in less than five minutes, and we moved locations.

We stopped in Central Park and Columbus Circle. In each place, I'd work on my laptop. Tweet something silly from my phone. We even talked to a few strangers walking by to see what they thought about a guy who "gets paid to wear t-shirts for a living," but alas, no one had a spaz attack about it. After about an hour of filming all over the city, my Reuters Times Square interview was done.

That December, when the IWYS Reuters story went live, it did actually go global as I had dreamt when I walked into their head-quarters. Media outlets from Croatia, Australia, Japan, London, France, Brazil, Italy, and many other countries reached out to do follow-up stories. So far, that Reuters story has been syndicated to over 80 countries, many of them running on their featured morning or evening news hours. By December 15, 2009, over 90% of the 2010 IWYS calendar had already been sold, and I had officially earned my world-class-nickname: The T-Shirt Guy.

ONLINE DATING (SORT OF . . .)

Another life-changing email came from a friend named Jessica Thomas (who owns page 107). Jessica worked for a local Jacksonville business magazine and, in 2009, asked me to talk on a panel for a business/marketing event (which I did, and I melted faces). Another email from Jessica later in the year was different, though.

In it, she referred me to the President of the Advertising Society at University of Florida to speak at one of their events, which I thought was pretty rad. I had given a few talks to high school and college students, and I always loved their spirit and enthusiasm. At the time, IWYS averaged somewhere between 300 and 500 emails a day, and it was rare that I could remember to respond to all of them (even for speaking engagements—terrible, I know). Needless to say (but I'm saying it anyway), I didn't respond to the invitation and neither did the other person on the email: Caroline Winegeart.

A few months later, I received an @ reply on Twitter from one such @ckelso. She asked me if I could follow her so that she could direct message (DM) me about a speaking opportunity. After

---

I bought page 32 as this is the age the author, and my wonderful son, will be when his first book is published! WAY TO GO, Jas. Love ya tons.

looking at her profile, I realized the name looked familiar, but after stalking Google (yes, you may be noticing a pattern), I still couldn't place her.

I clicked the follow button, and she sent me a message asking me if I'd be interested in speaking for the Ad Society at the University of Florida (where she was the President). *Ah-ha!* I remembered the email from Jessica that I never responded to! We exchanged a few direct messages, and I told her that because of how limited my time was, I was charging for speaking gigs—even Skype chats.

Charging for speaking gigs is a tricky topic, and you might be thinking, *"But Jason! It's a speaking gig to a bunch of college kids! Why would you charge money?"* The answer is this: my time. I was running a (more than) full-time business, and every hour in my day is valuable. Even if your time isn't maxed out right away, if you don't start charging for speaking gigs early on, it's like climbing an epic uphill (both ways in the snow) battle when you *do* realize you need to charge. Besides, I didn't know this Caroline person, and the date she asked me to speak was only a week away. Even though it was a relatively local event, I had to make it a valuable exchange for my time.

We sent a couple more messages back and forth and eventually settled that I would do the gig. When the date and time rolled around a week later, I hopped on Skype.

"Hi! Can you hear and see me?" Her face was slightly too close to the camera, but she was easy on the eyes, so I didn't mind the close-up. She was brunette, with a generous smile and a friendly voice. I sat on my modern brown couch in the IWYS office, and because of all the media and videos I'd done, I had my camera and lighting setup in front of me. In staring at Caroline's face as she adjusted the camera, I was surprised to see the video on the other end of the call, since most of these "appearances" are one-sided and don't link up their video.

"Yep, can you hear and see me?" I adjusted myself on the couch and checked again to make sure the video was framed up well.

"Yes, I can see and hear you! Hi Jason, it's Caroline and the UF Ad Society!" She waved and slowly backed away from the camera, revealing a few hundred college kids sitting in an auditorium.

"Hellooooooooo people." I leaned forward into my external microphone.

"Thanks so much for taking the time to talk to us! We've got you up on a big screen here, and we're ready to hear all about IWearYourShirt.com." She was the master of talking while walking backwards, making her way to a seat amongst the other students.

From there, I relayed to these college students how I had crafted this unique business idea, spending almost no money to start it, and telling a bunch of random stories about t-shirts I'd worn and things I'd done in the first two years of business. While I was talking, I couldn't help but notice myself looking at two people in the audience. One was the attractive brunette (Caroline), who must have flipped her hair about 20 times (and I noticed each one). The other was a young guy who was kind of scrappy looking (he reminded me of myself in college) and wearing a bright orange shirt.

> **Fun side note:** *The guy wearing that orange shirt was Burton Hohman (Burtle aka Burt aka the IWYS intern in 2011). Burt was the first person to ask a question after I was done speaking, and when he raised his hand, I called him "Orange Shirt Guy" (because I didn't know his name). That moniker stuck with Burt for nearly two years on the*

Internet. Everyone from the IWYS community knew Burt as the "Orange Shirt Guy." (Spoiler alert: Burt is not the reason this chapter is called online dating.)

When I finished my talk, Caroline came back close to the video camera and said thank you and goodbye. When I waved goodbye, all I could think was, "Man, if I had known this Caroline person was so attractive, I would have answered her email right away!"

After the call ended, I jumped into my inbox and crafted a witty reply to thank her for having me talk to the Ad Society. I giddily typed out the message in 30 seconds but left it open for about an hour before hitting send so I wouldn't seem desperate (you gotta play it cool!). It couldn't have been 10 minutes after I sent the email that Caroline wrote back telling me how great I was and that the students couldn't stop talking about IWYS. She also replied with some wit of her own, which I definitely took note of.

From those emails, Caroline and I kept talking on Twitter and a few times on the phone when she wanted to pick my brain about career options after college (a clever ploy I now realize was just to lure me in). That summer after she graduated, I found out she was coming back to Jacksonville, where she was conveniently from. We had our first lunch together at a burger place in Jacksonville Beach. Almost immediately after that lunch, we started dating. Six months later, she moved in with me. She's my partner in life and my best friend, but she's also one of the few people who truly understands how my crazy brain works. (Thank you, Caroline! I couldn't be where I am today without your love, your support, and your creativity!)

It just goes to show how important it is to answer your emails. So many unexpected opportunities came through my inbox throughout the course of IWearYourShirt.

Some of my closest friends to this day have come from intro-ductions and random emails I've received over the years. People I can relate to. People who go through the same struggles. People who aspire to "make a dent in the universe" (as my buddy AJ Leon says). When you're building a business, it's not only about making stuff happen, but it's also about taking advantage of opportuni-ties as they come to you. I always try to imagine that something exciting and life-changing is just around the corner. (And some-times, it is.)

Chapter 9

T-SHIRTS
+ LAST NAME
+ THIS BOOK
= $1,000,000

While I enjoyed success early on, IWearYourShirt certainly wasn't all puppies and rainbows when it was an active business from late 2008 to May 2013. I made some mistakes when it came to managing people and managing money, and not making tough decisions fast enough. That being said, I've learned countless life lessons from those experiences, and as painful as some of them were, I wouldn't go back and change them. Those experiences have helped me progress as a person and as a business owner, and they continue to provide value in my life.

Despite some of these hiccups, it's 100% true when I tell you that IWearYourShirt generated over $1,000,000 in revenue during its time, and I'm extremely proud of that. Most people (or media outlets) share business numbers like that and don't like to share the

The world's most beloved brands tell a bigger story. Learn how at www.GetStoried.com/core5

expenses that go along with that number. Let me be clear: I certainly don't have a cool $1M sitting in my bank account. Each year, I had expenses to pay. Both 2009 and 2010 were very profitable years for IWearYourShirt. The company made more money than it spent. In 2011 and 2012, the company unfortunately did not make more money than it spent. Yes, IWYS generated $350,000+ in 2011, but the expenses (salaries, website costs, promotions, etc.) were over $370,000. Some big changes were made in 2012 and 2013, and I realized that the business wasn't a scalable or profitable model the way I had been doing it, so I officially retired from "shirt wearing." Whether my financial situation was great or not so fantastic, I always tried to remind myself that at least *I* was in control of my life and running my own business the way I wanted to run it. That was the goal all along, even from the early days when I left the 9–5 world to start Thought & Theory.

However, if there's one simple business lesson I can impart to you from my ups and downs with IWYS over the years, it's to be diligent with your revenue projections and expenses. These things are constantly changing and evolving. You need to be on top of them or hire someone to be on top of them at all times. *And hey, if I can get brands around the world to pay me over $1,000,000 to wear t-shirts for a living, you can do anything!*

BUYMYLASTNAME

I've found myself on countless "Unconventional Ways to Make Money" lists. There was even a Cracked.com article in 2012 that named IWearYourShirt the "6th Least Impressive Way Anyone Ever Got Rich." While that title was a bit over the top, I've come to realize over the years that I take pride in doing things unconventionally.

// FROM JASON: Hey reader! Did you know I created a free app to help you easily find business hours? Go search "Storetime" in the App Store.

I embrace it. Doing things unconventionally has been the recurring theme for every single business venture I've started. Where people see rules and a standard way of doing things, I want to run in the opposite direction at a full sprint. Give me boundaries, and all I want to do is push beyond their limits, which is why in the fall of 2012, I found myself yet again sending out emails about a "crazy" idea I had. But before we get to that, let's back up a second.

In April 2012, my mom called me via Skype, which was not a normal occurrence, so I knew something was up. She told me that she and my stepfather were going to be getting a divorce—my stepfather whose last name I had taken. While he had been in my life for 13 years, my Mom was always the person I was closest to. On that call, I made a joke that I wanted to get a divorce, too, and I was going to *"sell my last name!"* That joke must have embedded itself in my subconscious because it eventually resurfaced in November of 2012 (and later in 2013) as BuyMyLastName.com. My idea was that I would legally take the last name of the high bidder. So if PlatypusDepot.com won the auction, I would legally become Jason PlatypusDepotdotcom for one year.

At the time, my sense of identity wasn't tied to my last name at all. Having multiple last names throughout your life will do that to you. Where I had found my greatest sense of self was through the Internet. As weird as that sounds, I built some of the strongest relationships I had by meeting people on Twitter and Facebook, through email and IWYS. So when I launched the auction to sell my last name in November 2012, I made sure one thing was absolutely clear: **It would be profitable!** I kept the expenses extremely low and only paid for website design and development and some PR help. The website design and development was less than $1,500, and the PR help was a percentage cut of the total last name sale (no up front money). There was also 10% of the final sale going to a charitable organization. So from the start, I knew that I would pocket at least 75% of the total revenue BuyMyLastName brought in. Look at me, learning from my mistakes!

In 2012, the first auction on BuyMyLastName kicked off with an amazing bang. Within the first 24 hours, the bidding was up over $30,000. I was stoked! After 40 days, Headsets.com won the last name auction for $45,500. I had zero expectations going into that crazy business idea, but I knew if nothing else, it would be profitable.

You may be wondering why a company would purchase someone's last name. Well, I banked on the fact that I had spent four long years building a reputation, accumulating a following, and gaining media attention online. I knew that companies wanted to pay me to wear their t-shirts, so I figured selling my last name was something a brand might be interested in as well for the exposure it could get them. After the auction ended, news of my last name sale spread like wildfire. The story of Headsets.com paying $45,500 for my last name was on the homepage of *USA Today*, CNN, CNBC, *Huffington Post*, and many more. Not only was the media attention good for Headsets.com, but they also reported an increase in sales of $250,000 in first few months of 2013. Bam! Not too shabby.

With the successful case study of BuyMyLastName in 2012, I decided for 2013 I would auction my name off one more time. The second auction would be exactly the same, except the big selling point would be the byline on the cover of the book you're currently reading. The second auction for my last name ended at $50,000 and was won by two budding entrepreneurs who built a free surfing app (download "Surfr" on your iPhone!). (At some point this year, I guess I should probably learn to surf, huh?)

As awesome as it was to put a profitable and successful feather

Single? Spritzr is the smarter way to date, connecting you to your single friends of friends – it's like being at a friend's party!

in my business cap, I think the possibilities that BuyMyLastName represents are even more awesome. It's an example of how many business opportunities exist but that people pass up because of the restraints of conventional thinking. At the time I thought of BuyMy-LastName, the IWearYourShirt model wasn't operating profitably. But I knew I had value to provide businesses in my audience and my reputation in spite of that fact. By opening myself up to any and all ideas (no matter how crazy), I was able to identify a $50,000 revenue opportunity for myself.

HOW I MADE $75,000 WITH CREATIVITY FOR SALE

When I finally decided I was going to write a book, you can imagine I didn't want to do it like everyone else. I have friends who are authors, and most of them talk about books as opportunities to create influence for yourself or to market your other products. Not very many of them talk about actually making money by selling copies of their books. Of course, being who I am, I saw this as a challenge. I knew I had a story to tell; now how could I make money doing it?

I'll leave all the "book publishing is broken" stories to people and authors who have more insight about it. Instead, I'll tell you exactly how I put $75,000 in my bank account before writing a single word of this book or selling a single copy.

STEP #1: CROWDFUNDING

I've been very curious about crowdfunding over the years. Sites like Kickstarter and Indiegogo are brilliant to me. I thought about using Kickstarter for my book initially, but when I started thinking about selling 200-page sponsorships (those super cool 140-character messages at the bottom of every page of this book), I realized Kickstarter probably wouldn't allow over 200 reward levels. That also seemed like a nightmare to set up and manage. So I set out to build my own crowdfunding website based on the idea that I would put small text advertisements on the bottom of the pages of my book, along with four larger sponsorship opportunities on the covers and inside cover flaps.

STEP #2: KEEPING EXPENSES LOW

Building a crowdfunding platform of your own can seem like a daunting (and expensive) task. Instead of spending oodles of money and trying to recreate Kickstarter, I sketched out a stripped-down version of a crowdfunding website. I didn't want to worry about fancy things like reward levels; instead, I'd look at selling my page sponsorships like you'd sell a product (t-shirt, mug, bag of coffee) on a website. With this mindset, I was essentially creating a fancy e-commerce website, and I could use my experience selling IWYS days as proof the concept worked. I reached out to my buddy Conrad Decker (who owns page 9 and 85) for his help with this project, and he agreed to help me build SponsorMyBook. com. While it may have looked like a complex website (if you saw it), it was actually just a custom designed Shopify theme. Huzzah! Internet magic!

STEP #3: SELLING 200 SPONSORSHIPS

On the day SponsorMyBook.com launched (learn more about my launch process in Chapter 19: Let's Do Lunch Launch), 50+ page sponsorships and both inside cover flaps were sold. In just 24 hours, I made $18,000 and my book didn't even exist yet. The launch went fairly smooth, but the page sponsorships didn't fly off the shelves like I'd hoped. What I realized quickly was that I was selling something intangible—something that had never been sold before. (If you're creating a business, I recommend you avoid selling this way; it's a difficult sell!)

Over the course of five months, I sent out over 1,200 emails to potential sponsors, not including multiple email blasts to my existing email lists. With a huge sigh of relief, all of the book sponsorships finally sold, and SponsorMyBook.com ended up netting me $75,000. It wasn't easy, though. Many times, I didn't think I'd find any other companies who believed in my story or this next crazy project of mine. And who would pay for a book they wouldn't see (or read) for months? But to me, it was worth all the hours and all the "No, thank you" emails I received. With exception to people who get huge book deals, I'm in a very small group of authors who actually make a profit from writing a book. I take great pride in that.

STEP #4: GOING FORWARD AND SELF-PUBLISHING

One of the biggest reasons I chose not to use a big book publisher with this book was because when I emailed Chris Brogan with the idea for SponsorMyBook, he so poignantly replied saying, *"Self publish your book, there's no reason to split your money with them (book publishers) for pathetic distribution."* That hit me like a slap in the face. Why on earth would I give any percentage of the profits of selling my book when I knew, as a first time author, a book publisher was barely going to help me sell copies of my book?

To put it in simple terms, would you rather sell 10,000 copies of a book and make 60% of the revenue or 20% of the revenue? I chose 60% and haven't looked back since. (The only reason I don't make 100% of the revenue is because I don't own a printing press and shipping company . . . yet.) Yeah, this book may never hit the shelves of Barnes and Noble, but I don't care because I can't force people to drive there, meander to the Business section, and look for my book amongst hundreds of others. But my book is on the front display of CreativityForSale.com, and I can drive thousands of people to that website for very little money and actually see sales (and profits!).

As we continue throughout this book, I challenge you to think about what value you provide and how you can think beyond how things may have been done before. Instead of seeing boundaries, learn to see opportunities to improve, to create, and to do unconventional things. There is always money to be made somehow, as long as you know the value you provide and you can identify the people who benefit from that value. Selling ad space on t-shirts and last names and the very pages of this book is proof of that fact.

Culture is not ping pong, mini fridges, catered lunches, or casual dress. It rises from the team & should bleed from leadership. www.PCR.is

SECTION 2: BUSINESS STUFF

Hopefully, you've learned a bit about how I turned virtually <u>nothing</u> into something of value, something people were willing to pay for. Now, I want you to discover what that is for you. The following section was written to help you formulate a business doing something that you love. For some of you reading this book, it may be rudimentary information. However, it's also possible that you may read something that sparks an entirely new, awesome business idea that brings you billions of dollars. You don't want to miss out on that, do you? I didn't think so. Read on my friend . . .

Have you seen BeautyAndBrains in Jason's book yet? Find us on pages 16, 36, 56, 68 and 136!

Chapter 10

FINDING YOUR NICHE TALENT

If you're reading this book, it *may* be because you're curious to learn more about me, and I'm happy to share my success (and failures) with you. However, I'm willing to bet you also want to help yourself. I'm hoping you're ready to grab your life by the horns and ride it into the sunset. And that's what this chapter is all about. Ready to shift gears?

By the end of this chapter, you should have a good grasp of what your creative superpowers are. Wait, do you have real superpowers? Can you turn any object into a stuffed platypus? Or maybe you have M-Ray vision (it's like X-Ray vision, except instead, everything you look at looks like macaroni-and-cheese)? Or do you have more common superpowers? Like the ability to write code and make a website actually function. Or the ability to turn a blank canvas into an amazing piece of art. Or you look at a sheet of music and play it masterfully in a few minutes. Let's take a look and explore what talent you have that you want to begin building a business around.

Creativity comes in all shapes and sizes, and for the purpose of this chapter, we're focusing on the creative talents you can use to

DeliFreshThreads.com is a tshirt brand inspired by the #KingofMeals, the SANDWICH. Check out my virtual deli shop & I'll pack you a sandwich.

make a living (read: make money). In my short time as a creative entrepreneur, I've really only worked on projects that I was happy to work on and that utilized skills I had at my disposal. It's my belief that entrepreneurship is exactly that: doing work that makes you happy with the skills you have. I'll do my best to help you find and hone your skills in this chapter.

The first thing you need to do is just take a deep breath. Go ahead and take one. Good. Now think about what skills or talents you have that are effortless for you and that you enjoy using.

Is it singing a beautiful song? How about coding a website? Are you a videographer and have a unique eye for composition? What about writing? Painting? Building stuff? Creating jewelry? Racing cars? Being a model? Responsive design? Playing a sport? Carpentry? Stand-up comedy?

The talent you *enjoy* is the one I want us to focus on together. Whatever you currently do for a paycheck, unless you're going to parlay that into a new job, leave it behind in your thoughts for now. If you don't have a job at the moment, that's perfectly okay, too. Focus solely on your talent.

Taking the steps to create a business or make side income doing something you enjoy will not only make you happier, but will also lead to your overall fulfillment. It's not going to be easy, but when you're doing work around something you actually enjoy, it won't feel like your current or existing work feels. Take it from me; I worked about ten different jobs before IWearYourShirt, and in just the first three months of IWYS, I was so much happier and felt a level of success I had never felt before, despite the fact that it was a roller coaster.

It wasn't about money, because I hadn't made more than my previous 9–5 job. But when I was able to strip away all standard things that felt like work (a corporate office, a terrible commute, a crappy boss, a 401(k), Excel spreadsheets, mundane meetings, etc.) and just focus on creating and building something with my talent, it was an amazing feeling—one I had never experienced before.

Now, let's look at your talent. Let's say you really enjoy filming and editing videos. Right now these could be home videos, videos of your family around the holidays, or just small things you've experimented with in iMovie. Congratulations, you're officially a videographer! Now what's unique about the way you do videography? Do you have a good eye for composition? Is there a special location where you always create outstanding video content? Maybe it's the beach? Maybe it's a specific person you film? Maybe it's a 50mm 1.4F lens you love? What are things you do as a videographer that set you apart from other videographers? Use this same thought process for whatever talent it is you're focusing on. **This is your niche talent.**

When you identify your niche talent, not only are you discovering something that would make you happy to do full-time, but you are also on your way to understanding the value you provide and (most importantly) how to turn that value into a substantial living.

Chapter 11

TURNING TALENT INTO MONEY

I've talked to hundreds of business owners, creative people, students, and aspiring entrepreneurs over the years, and the one thing that seemed to be the most common stumbling block to building a fulfilling business was this one question: I know what I *like* to do, but I have no clue why someone would pay me to do it. (Well, not with an attitude like that, they won't!) The key to unlocking the financial potential of your niche talent is about identifying your value—the thing that you offer the world. Once you figure that out, it's just a matter of learning how to price it so that people will pay for it. We'll talk about both in this chapter.

INDENTIFYING VALUE

So what is it about your niche talent that brings value to someone else? You may not think your talent or idea is capable of becoming a full-fledged business, but I started with the idea of getting paid to wear t-shirts for a living. Something tells me you might have a bit more than that in mind.

We roast fine coffees for the beautiful people of this world. We love stories, passion, and delicious drinks. Populace Coffee Love.

When thinking of ways that you can provide value to other people with your niche talent, ask yourself if your talent revolves around creating a product or a service. Do you have a specific skill that people would pay you to help them with? Are you particularly knowledgeable in an area that you could teach people about? Do you want to create something people buy once and use, or something people would pay a subscription fee for? Remember, it's all about identifying your **value** and then turning that into a reason someone would pay you (take BuyMyLastName, for example). Once you identify the value, you can think about pricing and monetizing your talent.

MONETIZATION

Pricing whatever product or service you want to sell can work a few different ways. One thing you want to make sure of is that no matter how you set up your pricing, the customer should be getting more perceived value than the price they paid would suggest. You want the customer to spend money, but you also want them to shout from the rooftops how happy they were that they bought your *stuff*. Let's look at a few examples of ways you can price your products or services that will help attract customers.

PRICING AS A MARKETING TOOL

What I did with IWearYourShirt was a perfect example of using pricing as a marketing tool. When I started, I had zero followers online. I had a dormant Facebook account. My Twitter account had fewer followers than I have toes on my feet. I knew I needed some unique hook to get people talking about IWYS, but more importantly, I needed to get people to buy days. The incremental, $1 per day pricing structure did exactly that. When people talk about IWYS,

Jason, nice work on the book! Be sure to follow @its_me_erich!

one of the first things they say is "And Jason created this incredibly unique pricing structure . . ."

My friend Chris Yeh helped come up with the pricing structure, but he and I were both inspired by someone else's project first: Alex Tew. Alex was 17 years old when he launched the infamous Million Dollar Homepage. I still remember getting the email from a co-worker at the ATP about it and being shocked. The Million Dollar Homepage was a website that was essentially a grid of one-pixel boxes. Each pixel was sold for $1, and if all of the pixels sold, it would net its creator, Alex, $1,000,000. It was genius. No one would just buy one pixel, because it was so tiny on the website so Alex made the minimum purchase a 10x10-pixel block for $100. Companies of all shapes and sizes bought different groups of pixels on the website so they could show their logo, which was clickable to their website (Fun fact: Alex's good friend was the first to buy pixels on the website and spent $400. Remember that "contact list" thing I talked about?). The Million Dollar Homepage was essentially thousands of tiny virtual billboards. By the time I saw the website, months after it had launched, it was nearly full.

MARKETING IS ALL ABOUT GETTING PEOPLE TO TALK ABOUT WHAT YOU ARE DOING.

The interesting part of the Million Dollar Homepage story that most people don't know is how Alex continued the momentum and pixel sales. After he sold the first $1,000 worth of pixels, he used that money to get a press release written. One press release was picked up by the BBC (Alex is from the UK) and shortly thereafter, a handful of other popular media outlets picked up the buzz and wrote about the site. Just two months after Alex launched the Million Dollar Homepage, he had sold over 500,000 pixels. Two months after that, it was reported that the Million Dollar Homepage was the

127th most visited website on the Internet. To put that in perspective, ESPN.com, the world's most popular sports website, is ranked around 100th each year).

The website was so popular that Alex announced the last 1,000 pixels would be sold on eBay, and the final auction price for those pixels ended at $38,100. When the final pixels sold, Alex had grossed over $1,037,100. After taxes and a large donation, he walked away with somewhere between $650K and $700K. Alex sold every pixel on the website and went on to become a household name in the online world in 2005–2006, which, as you remember, was before the social media craze.

Unique pricing structures, like IWYS and the Million Dollar Homepage, become a piece of marketing on their own. And marketing is all about getting people to talk about what you are doing. How can you sell your products or services in an interesting way? How can you think outside the box with your next business like Alex and I have been able to do?

THE FREEMIUM MODEL

Without knowing it, you've undoubtedly purchased products or services using the Freemium model. One of my favorite uses of this model is by a cloud storage company called Dropbox. In Dropbox, you sync a folder on your computer with the application, and it will create a duplicate set of files that's always up-to-date in the cloud. You can always access these files on your computer, with or without an Internet connection. If you make updates to your files or create new files on your computer, Dropbox will sync them automatically and make sure they're backed up.

When you initially sign up for a Dropbox account, it's 100% free, and they give you 2GB of storage space. For many people, this

"Luck favors the prepared mind. Practice and prepare and you'll be in it to win it." - Caron Streibich

is plenty of space to back up important documents, photos, and maybe some music files. However, if you're like me and have large design files, video files, etc., you'll need to upgrade from a free account to a premium account (ta-da! "Freemium").

I use the 200GB Dropbox account for $199 per year. While I do still use an external hard drive to back up my computer, I also like having a Dropbox account so that if I'm traveling, I never have to worry about losing new files I create.

Dropbox offers multiple premium account levels, ranging in price from $10 per year to $999 per year. But Dropbox has taken their Freemium model one step further. They offer a few free ways to increase your storage capacity simply by sharing Dropbox with your friends on social media or by referring friends to sign up for free accounts.

There are many instances of the Freemium pricing model. If you plan on using one, make sure to remember your value proposition. Give your customers something for free, but offer them something even more amazing if they pay a little bit of money.

VALUE TO SALE MARKETING SEQUENCE

I've seen value to sale marketing sequence (VSMS) in action more times than I can count, but I had no clue this pricing strategy had a name (thanks, Brendon Burchard).

The idea behind VSMS is that you give away some great content if people sign up for your email list. Once they're signed up and confirmed to your email list, you deliver the free content you offered. This content can be in the form of an e-book, an online course, a video series, a bunch of blog posts, etc. At the end of the free content, you offer people more in-depth content, similar to what they just consumed, for a fee.

Now that I've explained VSMS, you probably realize you've fallen right into someone's sales funnel on multiple occasions, right? I know I have. There are definitely a large group of people online who are doing VSMS in gross and less than desirable ways, and I won't name names. Instead, I want to share someone who does VSMS well in my opinion: my friend, Paul Jarvis.

Paul is a best selling author and an extraordinary designer and human being. Paul lives just outside of Vancouver, British Columbia, has a regal beard, two pet rats he rescued (you can see them on his Instagram account @pjrvs), and doesn't eat meat (my only problem with Paul). While planning to write this book, I came across his "My Damn Book" course (#mydamnbook and mydamnbook.com) and I signed up.

Paul sent my first lesson via email. I wasn't sure what to expect. Was this going to be like some of the other free courses I had signed up for over the years that made big promises but delivered nothing but sauerkraut (in my world, sauerkraut = crap)? Paul's course was nothing like any other I had ever signed up for. The email itself was well-designed, and Paul's writing was littered with sarcasm and expletives. I don't *love* expletives, but when I read Paul's phrase "be a fucking firehose of writing," I laughed out loud. By the time I finished reading the first email, I was smiling ear to ear. I was anxious to receive the next email from Paul and really pumped to start writing my book. His emails had great content and often ended with a question like "Why are you writing a book, and what value are you going to provide your reader?"

Lesson after lesson, I consumed Paul's emails like I consume red Skittles (which is voraciously, by the way). After eight lessons, I finished the #mydamnbook course and had a bunch of great notes and inspiration for the book you are currently reading.

And then "it" happened. I was sitting on my couch watching football when I received the final email. I had completed the #mydamnbook course, so I knew exactly what this email was; I had fallen right into Paul's sales funnel. Damn you, Paul. You wooed me with your book-writing knowledge and your Canadian humour (see what I did there?).

His email started with a simple question "Who made this course?!" It went on to talk a little bit about Paul, saying that he was a "gentleman of adventure" (I laughed out loud again). Then Paul listed three books he had published: *Everything I Know, Be Awesome at On-line Business*, and *Eat Awesome*. I looked at the links

HE HAD PULLED ME IN WITH HIS EMAIL MARKETING TRACTOR BEAM, AND THERE WAS NO CHANCE OF ESCAPE.

to those books and knew I had fallen right into Paul's VSMS trap. He had pulled me in with his email marketing tractor beam, and there was no chance of escape. Without hesitation, I clicked the *Everything I Know* link and was whisked away to Amazon.com to spend $11 on book containing everything Paul knew (note to Paul: I didn't buy the other books because I got everything you know in one book ☺).

I finished my purchase on Amazon and went back to Paul's email. For the first time in my life, someone offered a free course, delivered a ton of value, and converted me to purchase a product. I actually replied to that email and told Paul that he had won this Internet marketing battle but that the war was not over. Paul and I have since chatted on Skype a few times and his book *Everything I Know* is one of the easiest I've read. It's chock-full of inspiration and motivation to get out and do the thing you want to be doing in your life (much like I hope this book does).

· 56 ·

There are many examples of people doing VSMS like Paul—heck, you may have purchased this book from one of mine. You definitely don't have to have a book for VSMS. You can take the products or services around your niche talent and create a unique way to sell them with VSMS.

MULTIPLE PACKAGE PRICING

Have you ever visited a website, only to find yourself with multiple pricing options? Typically, there's a lower priced option that includes only the bare minimum (like a t-shirt). Then there's the middle price option that includes the lower priced stuff and a bit more (a t-shirt, some underwear, and some socks, for example). Then there's the mack-daddy pricing option that includes the lower priced stuff, the middle priced stuff, and 400,000 other products or services that you can't live without (t-shirt, undies, socks, shorts, hat, a hamster, Chinese food, two Ferraris, and more).

One person who seems to have mastered *multiple package pricing* is Nathan Barry. I've never met Nathan Barry, but I'm an avid follower on Twitter and have read a bunch of articles he's written. Nathan is a young software designer living in Boise, Idaho. He's made a name for himself by creating different information products on design, self-publishing, and website conversions—and all of them use multiple package pricing.

A recent post of his talked about pricing an e-book about web design. What Nathan did was start with a reasonably high price for his lowest package option (somewhere around $39). With this option, he promised that people who bought the product (an e-book with design tutorials in it) would learn skills to help them charge more for their time and products. Then, he added additional packages at higher price points, each one with more content and resources. The middle package was priced at $79 and included everything from the $39 package, along with additional web design resources, Adobe Photoshop files, and five video tutorials from Nathan. The highest package was priced at $169 and included everything from the $39 and $79 package, along with additional PDFs, a sample project, and a license to share (which meant you could pass everything along to 50 people). He named the packages: The Book + Resources, The Book + Resources + Videos, and The COMPLETE Package. These were sold on Nathan's website from lowest to highest priced.

Nathan had 322 total sales in 48 hours. He had 151 sales of the lowest package, netting $4,448; he had 104 sales of the middle package, netting $6,296; and he had 67 sales of the "complete" package, netting $8,803. You may notice he made twice as much money from the "complete" package as he did from the lowest package, with less than half the number of sales.

But Nathan wasn't done yet. For his next e-book product, this time about application (app) design, which was virtually the same content just repackaged, he consulted a friend and got some interesting feedback. That friend told him two things: (1) charge more, and (2) reverse the order in which the packages appear on the page. So he did. He changed the package pricing and the order, from $249 down to $99 and then to $39 (the lowest package price remained unchanged). This time, 48 hours after launch, Nathan had 404 total sales. And sales were up 25%, and his revenue was up 77% (it helped that he made an additional $150 per sale from the "complete package")!

Nathan learned a couple important things from his multiple package pricing. First, he learned that by offering multiple packages, he wasn't excluding any customers (even when he flipped the pricing from low-to-high to high-to-low). Customers knew they were interested in buying products by going to his website but didn't know they'd have multiple pricing options. They were already primed to make a purchase—now they just had to decide if they wanted all the extra bells and whistles (and who doesn't want extra whistles?).

Then Nathan learned that by flipping the packages from low-to-high to high-to-low, he could generate more revenue by increasing the total amount of "complete" package sales.

Nathan's example of multiple package pricing is just one of many. The crowdfunding platform Kickstarter was built entirely around the idea of multiple package pricing. Smart Kickstarter project owners will offer slightly more expensive rewards that include everything in the previous reward as the price increases. I've succumbed to this on many occasions with Kickstarter. I'll plan on spending $20 or $50 to back a project, but I end up spending $75 or $100 because the offer is just too good (damn you, Kickstarter projects!).

Multiple package pricing is a great way to offer additional value, so try not to limit yourself to only one product. Think about what you're selling. What additional things could you offer that could be packaged into other pricing levels?

You may find yourself starting with one type of pricing structure or monetization strategy and pivoting (as they say in the biz) to another one. This is perfectly okay. The most important thing to remember is that the product or service you sell needs to have a higher perceived value than the price you sell it for. In most cases, your product or service needs to make your customers a better version of themselves after they buy it. When I sell anything online, my goal is for people to share with the world what they just bought. How does that affect what you sell (or want to sell)?

Chapter 12

GETTING THE FOUNDATION RIGHT

When you're first starting to think about your business, it's easy to get caught up in the future and all your big aspirations. I think everyone needs goals to strive for, but you also need to lay the proper business foundation. It's important to take care of the simple things up front. If you don't, they can come back to bite you in the ass and kill those big aspirations. (Yeah, that's the tone of this chapter, so get used it.)

Now, I'm by no means a business expert, lawyer, or professional accountant. I just want to share my thoughts with you on some of the stuff you should get out of the way in the beginning, so you never have to think about it again and can focus on doing the awesome stuff you love!

YOUR BUSINESS STRUCTURE

Are you a Sole Proprietorship? A Limited Liability Company (LLC)? An S-Corporation (S-Corp)? A C-Corporation (C-Corp)? Or something else?

Imagine: You are 6 years old today. No gift. No card. Enter Cheerfulgivers.org. Every $10, 1 parent can give 1 child a Happy Birthday.

I know it can all seem a bit confusing, but the type of business entity you pick is definitely something you want to decide before you start doing any business or making any money. For my first year of IWearYourShirt, I was a sole proprietor. The business and I were one and the same. I received all profits from the business, but I was also liable for all losses and debts.

There are advantages and disadvantages for every entity that exists, so I *highly* recommend that you get a business lawyer to help you at this stage. There just happens to be one who sponsored a page in this book and helped me set up BuyMyLastName as an LLC (see Ruth Carter Law on page 162). It's worth it to talk to a lawyer like Ruth, especially one that's willing to help entrepreneurs and won't charge you a ga-jillion dollars (that's a trillion × a billion, in case you were wondering).

MONEY TALKS (AKA HIRE AN ACCOUNTANT)

Oh, accounting and bookkeeping. How do I love thee? Prior to launching IWYS, my taxes were easy. I was always an employee of somebody else. I worked. I received a paycheck. I didn't write anything off. I was issued a W2, and I did my taxes. That was it.

When you own your own business as a sole proprietor, LLC, S-Corp, C-Corp, or something else, things get more complicated. You no longer receive one nicely formatted W2 that you sign and submit. Now you have expenses, write-offs, 1099s, independent contractors, income taxes, blah, blah, blah.

Let me tell you about my finance management error, in hopes that you can circumvent making this same mistake. During the first year of IWYS, I comingled all my finances. I figured since I *was* IWYS, it didn't matter what credit card I used to buy things. It didn't matter if I just pulled money from PayPal into my personal account. And hey, no need to become an LLC, that's for *real* businesses, not my whacky social media marketing company I created out of thin air.

Apparently, the IRS didn't think that way. When tax time rolled around, I had companies asking for W9s (is that like WD-40?) left and right. I remember trying to use TurboTax and not having a clue how to input my income and expenses (or even what they were). And I had been paid through PayPal by corporate checks, personal checks—heck, one person even sent a $100 bill with a t-shirt. To say I was disorganized would be an understatement.

Luckily, my (extremely loving) mother has a background in corporate finance. After some *serious* cajoling, we sat down together and looked at my multiple credit card statements, my PayPal account, and my bank account, and started the tedious process of making sense of all my business versus personal spending. It was a freakin' nightmare.

For a week, my mom called me several times throughout each day, asking, "What is XYZ expense on your American Express?"

My normal response: "Uhh . . . No clue."

That didn't go over very well.

Fortunately for me, my mom stuck with it, and we were able to submit my taxes organized and on time. Immediately after finishing that ordeal, I got an accountant and IWYS became an S-Corp.

For the next few years, I paid $500 each year for an accountant, and it was a no-brainer. And the reorganization of income and expenses would drastically change and become more efficient (well, as efficient as it could be for someone who got paid to wear t-shirts).

My business mistakes may sound silly to you, but they're all too common. Because of the mistakes I've made and corrected, I've been fortunate enough to help many businesses over the years

These

through consulting. You'd be shocked at how many small business owners make these same errors.

Bookkeeping and taxes are not something *creative* entrepreneurs are inherently good at. Think about this way: would you rather worry about a 941 form that you need to file for self-employment (ew), or would you rather brainstorm how to land that awesome next client or create that badass new thing? Yeah. I'm choosing awesome client and badass new thing for you.

And consider this: when you hire an accountant to do the stuff that doesn't light you up, remember that you're contributing to them getting to do something that lights *them* up.

BUSINESS EXPENSES VS. PERSONAL EXPENSES

Whether it was buying packaging materials to send out t-shirts to fans or buying groceries, I used the same credit card and the same bank account with everything during my early stages of IWYS. Nothing was separate, and it was a *nightmare* to deal with. (Okay, so it was a nightmare for my mom to deal with when she had to do my bookkeeping in 2009 . . . thanks again, Mom. Love you!).

Almost any bank will set you up with a free business checking account these days, which includes a debit card and checks. You might just be starting with no plans to make money for months, but you should absolutely get a separate business account. The same goes for your credit cards.

REALLY? EVEN MY CREDIT CARDS?

There are stacks of books written on using credit cards wisely and not going into debt. Since I am someone who went into *serious* credit card debt, heed my advice: avoid using a credit card at all

messages

costs. Use your business debit card for business expenses if you can.

I understand that sometimes you need to use credit to take risks and get through tough times. I know; I've been there.

But whatever you do, don't get caught up in the hype of credit card rewards, cards that offer cash back, yadda yadda yadda. This stuff is all marketing BS and should be ignored unless you've had a ton of experience using credit cards and an equal amount of self-control. The rewards they offer are almost *never* worth it. You have to spend an obscene amount to get any kind of decent reward. I remember when I spent (and paid off) my first $30,000 on my company credit card. The amazing reward I racked up? A flight voucher worth $300 that I could barely use due to restrictions and blackout dates. Talk about a freaking bummer.

Get a credit card with the lowest APR you can find, and only use it if you *absolutely* have to. Staying debt-free is one of the best things you can do as a business owner. When I was under serious credit card debt, it loomed over me like a dark storm cloud. Every. Single. Damn. Day. It takes a mental toll on you and robs your brain of precious creative thinking. Hopefully, I've made my point? (I'm happy to share stories about credit debt over more tequila.)

DEBT AND THE ADJUSTMENT OF MY PRIORITIES

As I mentioned, I've gone into debt, I've come out of debt, and I've gone back into debt. I haven't *always* made poor financial decisions over the years, but in hindsight, I could have bootstrapped it more. All profits go back into a business, and all expenses are kept at an extreme minimum.

One of the bigger mistakes I made over the years was a simple one: I used a company credit card (because I had a huge credit

are

limit and "credit card perks") to pay for *all* my business travel and expenses. I was bad at paying the credit card down immediately with money from the corporate checking account. It wasn't that I didn't have the money to spend; it was that I simply didn't take the time to move money around and pay down the credit card balance.

Not paying off the credit card right away came back to bite me in the ass when the business went through rough times and I got low on cash. Had I paid off the credit card when I should have, I would have seen the low cash flow situation sooner. If I would have been cognizant of the situation earlier, I might have adapted the business model to make more money (or spend less money on fewer employees). Either way, I learned a valuable lesson. If I absolutely must use a credit card, I pay it down as quickly as possible.

For the past few years, I haven't touched my corporate credit cards. I use a business debit card and a personal debit card. It keeps things organized, and I never have to worry about interest on purchases or more debt piling up on me. It's liberating to not have a credit card burning a hole in my wallet.

GULP . . . GET A LAWYER

Throughout the life of my business, let's just say I've encountered a few sticky situations when it was beneficial to have a good lawyer in my back pocket. This is definitely something I'd recommend, even if you think you're *positive* you won't need it. And something to think about with that lawyer: Make sure it's someone you know, someone you've been referred to, or someone who has a track record you trust. Lawyers are expensive and often confusing, but they're damn good at writing contracts and keeping you from getting in trouble when you slip up.

blank

GET EVERYTHING IN WRITING

Man, oh man, this is one of those business lessons that is absolutely essential—whether it's getting contracts in writing from your clients or vendors, or written agreements between co-founders or employees and contractors. Verbal agreements (almost) never work out, and I've had a few of them end terribly (I'll happily share stories over more tequila).

Shake Law (Shake), is a free iPhone app that makes writing contracts simple, especially when dealing with agreements that would normally be verbal. Let's say you barter your design services for a one-page advertisement in a local magazine. In a matter of seconds, you can use the Freelance template on Shake and create a legally binding agreement between you and the magazine. Once created, the app will email a link to the contract, and it can be signed with one simple click. Shake has agreement templates for Freelance, Confidentiality, Bills of Sale, Renting/Lending, and Money Loans. Shake also gives you the ability to create your own agreement, say, if you wanted to shave all the luxurious locks of hair off your hands, and in return, I gave you a grilled cheese sandwich. I know it sounds weird, but hey, we agreed "hair for sandwich," and I don't want you backing out on me.

Like all things legal, Shake will tell you that their agreements are 100% legally binding. They're just like any other contract you'd write up, but you should consult a lawyer if you're dealing with high-stakes transactions or selling your company. If you're looking to write up a contract between you and the co-founder of your company, you could definitely use Shake. Even still, I'd recommend you involve an outside party who has experience in writing those terms so both of you are completely covered. And trust me, you

on

could get into business with your bestest-bestie-best-BFFL-friend ever, and something will undoubtedly happen. The short version: get it in writing.

INVOICING AND BILLING

One word: Freshbooks.

I've been using Freshbooks.com's online invoicing service since 2009, and it's worth its weight in gold bullion.

If you only have one client that pays you, great! Freshbooks is free with one client. Up to 25 clients? It costs $19 a month. Have 10,000,000 clients? $39 a month.

Seriously.

With Freshbooks, you can create professional looking invoices in a matter of minutes and you don't need to have any design or technical skills. Once you send invoices, Freshbooks makes it easy to send reminders for those pesky clients that take forever to pay. There is also a full accounting dashboard that will show you paid invoices and outstanding invoices.

The other great thing about Freshbooks? It's a cloud company (oooh . . . ahhhh . . .), which means they store everything online. You don't have to keep any invoices on your computer or in those big ugly metal filing cabinets. Freshbooks can also handle your expense tracking, time tracking, balance sheets, and other cool stuff.

I've done invoicing through other companies, one of which rhymes with SchmayPal, and it just doesn't compare to the ease of use of Freshbooks. Plus, they have a quirky team and their customer service is top notch. They definitely get the Jason SurfrApp seal of approval!

purpose. Find your inner rebel at www.therebelwithin.us

Okay, I think we've hit some sort of maximum limit on boring material with mentions of the IRS, invoicing, *and* lawyers in this chapter, so I'll just wrap it up by saying this: these things are essential to building a strong foundation for your business to sit on. It can seem intimidating if you've never dealt with any of it before, but I learned everything I know through trial and error and simply asking other people for help. I know you can do the same.

Chapter 13

PUTTING THE RIGHT PEOPLE IN PLACE

When it comes to your business, the people you surround yourself with can make or break you. The right people can help give you important feedback, get you exposure, bring in sales, and help you gain credibility quickly. The wrong people can run a business into the ground, create unnecessary negativity, and hold you back from doing something great. Be very picky and methodical with who you include in your business.

YOUR CO-FOUNDER

You may be the first co-founder (your idea) or the second co-founder (your friend's idea and you jumped on board), but either way, you're basically married. Now, I haven't been married, but I get the gist: 'til death do us part, through sickness and health, etc. When you're an entrepreneur, having a co-founder can be the best thing ever or . . . the worst thing ever. When the business is doing well, you can share the success together, or success can tear co-founders apart. When the business is in the crapper, you can both focus on

This page sponsored by TacoLu, home of fish tacos, Tequila and Mezcal! But really, we're just a front for the Jason SurfrApp fan club.

fighting your way out of it, or the crapper can tear co-founders apart. Either way, you're in this thing together and should embrace that fact.

Back when I was a co-founder of Thought & Theory, I remember how great it was to have someone to lean on and work with. It's an entirely different dynamic when you have a co-founder and you're not just an employee or independent contractor.

Again, the first thing you should do if you have a co-founder is get something in writing that clearly states several things. If you're already on it, you'll have to address the following, in writing, *with someone who writes contracts*:

1. What is each person's role in the company? Who is the CEO? Who is the CMO? Do you need those types of titles? What are the main things each person is going to be doing for the company daily?

2. If the business is an LLC, what percentage of the company does each person own? If it's an S-Corp (or C-Corp), how many shares of stock does each person own? Is there a vesting period when that percentage or those shares are available? What happens to ownership in case of investors?

3. What are the general expectations of each founder? What skills or abilities is each person contributing to the company?

4. Can each person cash out his or her percentage or shares at any time? Does there have to be an event (funding, acquisition, etc.) to cash out?

As you can see, co-founders need to think about many questions before getting started. The very beginning is the best time to have these discussions. It would help to bring in a lawyer or a business mentor to help work through these questions.

When the business hasn't had any success or failures, co-founders are much more amicable to each other. The last thing you want is to be scrambling to figure out who owns what percentage of the company while you're searching for investors or have a buy-out opportunity. Just remember, you're in this thing together. Work together, have lots of open discussions, and don't be afraid to ask for help from a mentor if you don't think things are going swimmingly.

MENTORS

You may remember Chris Yeh from earlier in the book. He was a great mentor for me. He offered tons of advice when it came to organizing my business, pricing and strategy, and connecting me with influential people.

Another mentor that's been great for me in recent times is Shane Mac. Shane has a ton of business experience, especially as it relates to growing companies and raising capital. He lives in the heart of Silicon Valley, knows virtually *everyone*, and is actually younger than I am.

When you think of a mentor, you typically think of a gray-haired older person who's been around the block, right? Well, mentors come in all shapes and sizes, and the most important thing when trying to find them is that you feel comfortable with them, that you trust them, and that they believe in you.

Let's get real for a second. Mentors are glorified, unpaid business therapists. They take their knowledge and experience, and they share it with you whenever you're in need. With some mentors, you can pick up the phone and call them on a whim, like I can with

Shane. And then some mentors you don't talk to very often, but they're only an email away, like Chris Yeh.

YOUR TRUST CIRCLE

I stumbled into having a trust circle in 2012. I had built relationships with people through social media, through attending conferences, and through wearing t-shirts for them, and I felt a certain level of trust in them. When the idea for BuyMyLastName appeared in my crazy marketing brain, I knew exactly who to share it with first.

Building a trust circle is not difficult. These people are, most likely, already in your life and helping you. I find it important to establish the relationship with them ahead of time and let these people know you'd like to be able to count on them for honest and speedy feedback. My trust circle is only 12 people, and I sent each person a very simple email asking if it'd be okay if I bounced ideas off them whenever they come to me. No one said "No" because the trust was already built. If you do find that people say "No" when building your own trust circle, don't harbor any ill will toward them—just move on to the next person. Your trust circle can be as little as three or four people or as many as 20.

I expect my trust circle to do these four very important things:

1. **Respond quickly.** This is honestly the most important thing for my trust circle. Sometimes you get an idea and want to move on it quickly. These people are an email or text message away, and they always respond swiftly.

2. **Be more than just yes/no people.** My mom and my grandmother are not in my trust circle (as silly as that sounds). This

72 is the average number of heartbeats per minute for a resting adult. #knowledge

is because they love me to death and will support any crazy thing I come up with. Your trust circle shouldn't be people who are going to pat you on the back. It should be people who are going to massage your back for hours (not literally—well, okay maybe). I purposely don't have close friends or family in my (business) trust circle.

3. **Give me brutally honest feedback.** While I want quick and honest feedback, I also want more from their feedback than just a "yes" or a "no." I want business acquaintances that I trust and respect to say, "Jason, this idea sucks. What about this . . . ?"

4. **They're in different industries.** The people in my trust circle are best selling authors, entrepreneurs, artists, marketing coordinators, fashion designers, bloggers, and more. I love that they're all different, because they all offer a unique perspective. It's also a plus when they all think an idea is awesome.

Notice I didn't say anything about buying, sharing, or offering any type of fulfillment with my mentors or trust circle. Your trust circle is *brainpower*. It's feedback. It's a group that has a diverse set of experience from which you can learn. You won't build your trust circle overnight, but you also don't need 12 people either.

In all likelihood, you have three or four business acquaintances right now (even through friends of friends) who would be willing to help you. Also, and this is important, *you don't need to tell these people they're in your "trust circle."* That might weird some folks out. Instead, just let them know you'd love to have them on call for feedback and thoughts on your business (or life).

And one last thing: these people shouldn't expect anything from you in return. Remember, this group is built completely on trust for you.

Chapter 14

WHAT DO YOU NEED?

Now that we've talked about how you're going to make money and covered the basics of setting your business up with the right foundation, you're probably wondering what you need to actually get started and find some customers.

WEB DESIGN AND DEVELOPMENT: YOU GET WHAT YOU PAY FOR

Having a solid website to promote your product or service is absolutely key. It's your hub of information. It's your sales platform. It's the one place people can come learn all about you and what you do. If you don't already have a website, get one.

There are hundreds, maybe *thousands*, of hotel chains in the world. When you pay for a cheap hotel, you expect it to be cheap. The bedspread will mostly like be some floral pattern, and you'll want to sleep wearing your clothes to avoid catching any diseases.

The bathroom will be small and dingy. There's usually ugly and dated carpet and an old tube TV on top of particle-board furniture. When you get up in the morning for breakfast, you assume there's a continental breakfast (which is just a fancy way of saying powdered

 treehouse™

LEARN THE SKILLS TO LAND YOUR DREAM JOB, EVEN WITHOUT A DEGREE.

Start learning with your
free trial today!

PLEASE NOTE:
THIS BUTTON
DOES NOT
ACTUALLY CLICK

This is a cool video from Treehouse that talks about learning valuable web design, development, and business skills.

Go to jointreehouse.com/jason to watch it.

ps. When will someone invent paper that plays videos??

eggs and tiny boxes of cereal). But you expect these things, because you know you aren't paying much for the hotel room.

On the flip side, when you book an expensive hotel room, you expect it to feel luxurious. The bed will have sheets on it that are over two billion thread count. The room will have a flat screen TV with more channels than you'll know what to do with. The bathroom **YOU GET WHAT YOU PAY FOR.** will have a giant bathtub you can imagine taking a bubble bath in, but most likely won't because grownups don't typically take baths (especially in strange places). There's a clear expectation when it comes to hotels: You get what you pay for.

Now, if you need web design or web development services, it can feel like the damn Wild West. Most likely, you'll have a friend of a friend who knows a lady who does "web design on the side" (which affectionately means she uses those crappy template websites and creates a logo for you in Microsoft Paint). You might also know someone who works at a large advertising agency with a starting price for a website of $10,000. Then there's everything in between. It can be difficult to make a decision on who to trust, but one thing rings 100% true: You get what you pay for.

In the middle of 2012, IWearYourShirt went through a downsizing, and the current website didn't service the new direction for the company. I had to get a new website made, but money was tight. For the first time, I decided to skimp on paying for a reputable company to build the website for me and instead I used one of those "design auction" companies. If you haven't heard of these, the idea is simple. You pay an upfront fee of, let's say, $499 to get a website built in 30 days. You typically include a design brief, which I was very thorough about and even included some hand-drawn website layouts I thought would be helpful.

Once you start your design auction, multiple freelance design-ers from around the world will flock to your project and pump out designs for you. Previously I had always used design companies I knew, designers I was referred to, or companies that my friends had used for their projects. This time, I stepped into the Wild West to try to save a few bucks.

The first week should have been a clear indication of what I was going to get for the $499 price I signed up to pay. It was crap—I mean, some of the worst web design I had ever seen (and I'd seen some terrible web design over the years). The color palettes these designers chose weren't anywhere close to the ones I had shared (and that were used in my logo). The design layouts didn't resem-ble the sketches I had shared and weren't functional at all. Some of the designs felt like someone just closed their eyes and clicked the mouse a bunch of times in a Photoshop file. With each design submitted, I was more and more frustrated.

To say I was disappointed would be an understatement. Here I had expectations of the web design I was used to, but I thought I could get that same quality at a fraction of the price. I was wrong. As the weeks went on, it was clear I wasn't going to get what I wanted (and had paid much more for). This shouldn't have been a surprise to me, but it was definitely a reaffirmation. I ended up cancelling the web design auction just in time to save a portion of my money. I took the remaining money and my disappointment back to a web designer I had worked with in the past whose price I was now happy to pay. That web designer cranked out work that was exactly what I had hoped for, and while I had to pay a lot more money for it, I was much more satisfied with the end result.

I've had similar situations when it comes to web development, too. I tried to go the cheaper route and always ended up with poorly written code (which other developers were happy to point out) and websites that didn't function properly. You wouldn't book a room at a Motel 6 and expect it to look like a Four Seasons. Whether it's web development or web design (or a hotel), you truly get what you pay for. The best advice I can give is to invest good money in your website working with someone you know and trust or that comes highly recommended. By doing that, you'll have the absolute best chance at getting a kick-ass website that does exactly what you'd hoped.

No matter who you work with, remember to start with the bare minimum. That bare minimum should still look amazing, but you just don't need every feature, bell, and whistle when you're getting started. The way your website works (usability) and looks (interface) are critical for creating a great first impression.

YOUR CONTACT LIST IS YOUR HOLY GRAIL

In the beginning of IWearYourShirt, I didn't really gain any traction or sales until I dug into my contact list and sent personalized emails to people. **Resist your initial impulse to immediately jump to social media websites to launch your project.** Instead, start with the network you already have (and that already trusts you). Trust is key when you're first getting started.

Whether it's making a purchase, signing up for an email list, downloading a product, or paying you for services, who do you think might be the first people to do those things? It's certainly not the non-existent audience you have on social media.

And even if you *have* grown some semblance of an audience, have you built trust and context with them for years? Aspiring business owners should organize their contact list and use it as a launching pad. *Get personal with your personal contacts.* Don't be afraid to ask for help. And don't oversell in the beginning. Feedback can be just as valuable as capital when getting started.

A friend of mine, Web Smith, co-owns a men's clothing company called Mizzen+Main. Two and half years ago when Web started, he had huge aspirations to sell high-quality men's dress shirts and blazers. Mizzen+Main's differentiating factor for their men's products comes from Web's co-founder Kevin Lavelle. Kevin attended Oxford University (so he's way smarter than me) and has experience in manufacturing and technology. Web and Kevin had an idea for the perfect men's performance blazer. The blazer could be thrown in a duffel bag, endure travel, and come out completely wrinkle-free and ready to wear. They also wanted to make sure this blazer had built-in stretch technology, so that men could wear it on the go.

They launched their company with a handful of impressive dress shirts and worked on their perfect blazer behind the scenes. The first edition wasn't up to their standards. And neither was the second. Or the third. Or the fourth. Two and half years later they had finally created the five iterations of the perfect blazer and it was just that: *perfect*. With two and a half years of experience building their brand and building a customer base, Mizzen+Main launched their "0-5 Blazer" with a Kickstarter project. They had already built a following on social media and a customer list, but you know what they did first? They reached out to their personal contact list (I was one of those people) and shared the Kickstarter project. They went directly to the people they knew trusted them and would help them spread the word.

With an initial goal of raising $15,000, Mizzen+Main destroyed their funding goal. After the first 24 hours of their 30-day Kickstarter project, they raised $30,000. At the conclusion of their crowdfunding effort, they had raised $54,568.

It's important to recognize the value of trust and relationships when you're starting (and) running a business. Focus on nurturing your contact list; it's one of your most important assets—if not *the* most important.

Nautilus Surf created the Adventurer: The first practical surfboard case. Learn more and start your adventure at nautilussurf.com

Chapter 15

DELIGHTING YOUR CUSTOMERS AND CLIENTS

Customer service is necessary in almost every business. Depending on whether you're selling a product or providing a service, customer service could include product support, loyalty rewards, or just building great relationships with your clients. If there's one thing I know, it's that great customer service is key to being successful no matter what industry you're in.

Great customer service can also be one of your best marketing tools. A great example of this is what LEGO did in 2013. Longtime LEGO fan Luka Apps, a seven-year-old from Britain, spent all his Christmas money on a Ninjago LEGO Ninja toy named Jay ZX. Against his father's advisement, Luka brought his Ninjago on a shopping trip. During that trip, Luka lost the precious Ninjago that he'd spent all his money on. You can imagine how devastating losing a toy is for a seven-year-old, especially a huge LEGO fan like Luka.

Luka didn't have any more money to buy a replacement Ninjago, so instead he wrote a letter to LEGO explaining that he had lost his new action figure. Here's the letter he wrote:

Hello.

My name is Luka Apps and I am seven years old.

With all my money I got for Christmas I bought the Ninjago kit of the Ultrasonic Raider. The number is 9449. It is really good.

My Daddy just took me to Sainsburys and told me to leave the people at home but I took them and I lost Jay ZX at the shop as it fell out of my coat.

I am really upset I have lost him. Daddy said to send you a email to see if you will send me another one.

I promise I won't take him to the shop again if you can.

—Luka

What happened next is a stroke of marketing genius, disguised as good customer service. A LEGO support representative named Richard wrote Luka back, but not before consulting a special someone. Here's the letter Luka received from LEGO:

Luka,

I told Sensei Wu [a Ninjago LEGO character] that losing your Jay mini figure was purely an accident and that you would never ever let it happen ever again.

KingdomDrivenEntrepreneur.com is an online community for entrepreneurs of faith who seek to build a thriving business.

He told me to tell you, 'Luka, your father seems like a very wise man. You must always protect your Ninjago mini figures like the dragons protect the Weapons of Spinjitzu!'

Sensei Wu also told me it was okay if I sent you a new Jay and told me it would be okay if I included something extra for you because anyone that saves their Christmas money to buy the Ultrasonic Raider must be a really big Ninjago fan.

So, I hope you enjoy your Jay mini figure with all his weapons. You will actually have the only Jay mini figure that combines 3 different Jays into one! I am also going to send you a bad guy for him to fight! Just remember, what Sensei Wu said: keep your mini figures protected like the Weapons of Spinjitzu! And of course, always listen to your Dad.

The story of Luka, his lost Ninjago, and LEGO's amazing response quickly spread through mainstream media and social media. Sites like Forbes, The Huffington Post, AdWeek, MSN, and many more shared this amazing customer service story. It wasn't a planned marketing campaign from LEGO, and I'm guessing it cost LEGO less than $10 to send Luka a new Ninjago and a few other toys. The amount of exposure they gained by doing great customer service was tremendous. I'm willing to bet it wasn't the first (or last) time LEGO has offered such great service to its customers; this story just happened to be one that everyone wanted to share. When I think about what LEGO did for this seven-year-old boy, it makes me wonder why more companies don't focus more on customer appreciation and less on customer acquisition. Sure, LEGO is a big, well-known brand, but there are stories like this with companies of all shapes and sizes. The key here is to realize that laying a great foundation of customer service can do more (and cost way less) to grow your customer base than any banner ad campaign or paid marketing stunt.

The way I was raised, my mom always made me treat other people with respect. The old golden rule: "treat people how you want to be treated," was repeated to me many times while growing up, and I'm glad it was. With every business I've owned, I've tried to go above and beyond to make customers, clients, and fans happy. If that meant giving someone a refund last minute because they had an unfortunate financial situation, I did it without hesitation. If that meant sending someone a different size t-shirt (at no cost to them) in the mail because they thought they were going to be a size Medium but actually needed a Large, I did it without hesitation. There was one question I always asked myself when it came to dealing with a customer service issue of any kind:

"How would I want to be treated in this situation?"

Once I started asking myself that question, I always knew what the right answer was. Even if I was handling a customer service situation with someone who wasn't friendly or nice, I was always as accommodating as possible. Kill 'em with kindness right? This leads me to my next point about keeping your customers or clients happy.

MANAGING EXPECTATIONS

For the most part, the beginning of IWearYourShirt went well as a business. It generated revenue, it was profitable, I enjoyed what I was doing, the companies I was wearing shirts for gave me great feedback, my community was growing, and I hadn't burned anything down or [yet] gotten kicked out of a Las Vegas casino for filming video at a blackjack table (*whoops!*). It seemed like the more

I created content and focused on IWYS, the more positive attention the business was getting. However, there are certain things I learned the hard way.

Early on in 2009, the IWearYourShirt website didn't have very much traffic. Because of that, I sold people on the idea and what I would be delivering (social media content). Then traffic started coming in. Within months, IWYS had 100,000+ visitors each month. This type of traffic isn't crazy, but it's fairly sizeable. I used the traffic as a way to sell companies that were interested in buying a day on IWYS.

When the traffic poured in, I saw it as something I could additionally sell. Some of the companies I had worn shirts for said their day with IWYS brought more website traffic and sales than they'd had the entire previous month. When I heard those stories, I wanted to share them and use them. The problem with that, however, is that web traffic and sales are not something you can 100% control.

When I told a potential IWYS buyer that they would see over 1,000 visitors to their website on their day, what do you think happened? They expected 1,000 visitors to their website on their day! This created some disappointed buyers. They weren't disappointed in the content I created and the unique way I shared their brand, but they didn't get the web traffic I had told them they would get. It took a few less-than-stellar emails from IWYS buyers until I realized I should go back to selling what I could control: social media content creation. If companies asked how much traffic they could expect, I would share stories of previous buyers but make it explicitly known that they shouldn't think that was going to happen to them (it was a bonus). And what do you think happened? IWYS buyer expectations were lowered when it came to web traffic, and

LakeSuperiorBrewing.com is Minnesota's oldest micro brewery and is proud to have lead Duluth's craft brewing renaissance since 1994. Cheers!

these companies were no longer sending me emails about web traffic disappointment. There's an old adage that I've tried to stick to since 2009:

UNDER PROMISE AND OVER DELIVER.

Write that in your notebook. Rip this page of my book out and tape it to the wall in your office. Whatever you need to do to remember that phrase, do it.

FIRE YOUR BAD CLIENTS, *IMMEDIATELY*

A "bad client" can be defined as many things. It can be someone who has unrealistic goals that will never think you're doing enough work. It can be someone whose expectations greatly outweigh the price they're paying for the product or service you're offering. And some bad clients are simply people who don't have a clue how to run their business and no matter what you do, you aren't going to be able to fix that.

In 2009, I ran into my first bad client, disguised as a small business owner of a beef jerky company. Now, I should preface the next few paragraphs with something very important: I. Love. Meat. There isn't a meal I have throughout the day that doesn't involve copious amounts of meat. And beef jerky? I eat it by the package, not by the handful. So you can imagine my mouthwatering excitement when I found out I'd be wearing a shirt for a beef jerky company. Like the majority of 2009 IWYS buyers, the owner of this dehydrated package meat company sought me out and was hoping IWearYourShirt would provide some exposure in their growing company.

AtlanticInkCrew.com is ready to rock out some hand-crafted, screen-printed apparel for you. Start your next printing voyage - ink or swim!

After exchanging a few emails, and going above and beyond to help the owner of the company create and print a shirt (in 2009, I had everyone send me their own shirts), the owner said they'd be sending me a box of beef jerky to enjoy throughout their IWYS day. I will admit that a few emails raised some red flags, especially one asking how many orders they could expect on their day. I learned very early on with IWYS that I had to stick to telling people they were getting exposure on social media and photo/video content. Sales of the products on my t-shirt were not something I could guarantee or even guess at.

The beef jerky day finally arrived and I was excited. I hadn't opened any of the beef jerky yet, as I wanted to do a live taste test on my Ustream live video show. From the time I woke up in the morning, I stared at these beef jerky packages. I told people on Facebook and Twitter about all the different flavors I had received. My own grandmother was excited that I was wearing a t-shirt for a beef jerky company and let me know she had bought a bunch that morning. When 3:00 p.m. rolled around, I started my Ustream show, and hundreds of IWYS fans tuned in (along with the owner of the jerky company). For the next hour, I opened and tasted nearly 10 pounds of packaged jerky. There was ostrich jerky, turkey jerky, beef jerky, buffalo jerky, and a bunch of other flavors and types of meats. As I tore each package open, I would smell the jerky and share with the audience what it smelled like. I'd pull a slice of jerky out and talk about the texture and the up close smell, and then take a bite. With each piece I ate, I tried to be honest about the flavor and texture. I remember the ostrich jerky being a bit chewier than the turkey jerky but still being packed with flavor. One of the spicier packages of jerky was oilier than the rest, and I commented about it. I didn't say "Ewwwwww, this is oily!" I simply stated it had a bit more oil than the rest but took a bite and described that it wasn't too spicy and still had great flavor. With each bite of jerky, I was descriptive but also positive. Even if one of the flavors wasn't my favorite, I never said anything negative about it. Eating the venison jerky was the first time I had ever tried venison (I'm sorry, Bambi!), so that was an interesting experience for me. Oh, and while I consumed multiple pounds of jerky on live video, I was also telling people where they could go to buy it.

Many people watching commented that they were buying it, had bought it, or were going to buy it later in the day. The entire time I was on video, the owner of the company was interacting on the live video chat (where everyone talked while I was on video). He seemed happy and excited to meet a bunch of potential new fans. After an hour of eating jerky, I had started to slip into a meat coma (we've all been there), and I finished the live show and went off air. I figured I had done a great job, had sold a bunch of jerky for this IWYS sponsor, and had enjoyed doing a unique jerky tasting on live video.

I figured wrong.

About 10–15 minutes after I went off air, I received an email from the beef jerky company owner. He was unhappy with how I talked about the jerky, didn't feel I "sold" it enough, and was disappointed with the company's IWYS day. My jaw dropped. I was still in a bit of a meat coma, but I was aware enough to be thoroughly stunned. This person had spent $162 to have me wear a t-shirt and promote his company, and I knew the company had at least made its money back—if not double what it spent (which was never even something I promised or talked about). I replied that I was sorry and asked if there was anything I could do to make it right. I also asked if additional sales came in thanks to over 1,000 people learning about the company on live video. He responded that sales increased but not nearly what he had expected. He also said he assumed I would be doing much more promotion, telling people to buy and saying all of the jerky was delicious. What had I just done for an hour on live video? I easily could have taken this opportunity to fire back an email and talk about all I'd done, but I could tell this person wasn't going to be swayed. I simply wrote back something along the lines of "I'm terribly sorry you feel this way, and I tried to represent your company in the best way I could, being as honest as possible. I also know a bunch of people purchased your products, including my own grandmother." His response was not friendly, stating "I will not be recommending IWearYourShirt and feel like this was a waste of my money." Again, I was stunned.

At that moment, I realized this was my first bad client. This person had unrealistic expectations, which I tried to manage up front. He was obviously not going to be happy with anything I said and had made up his mind. I took it upon myself to take the high road and refund the money he had spent on their IWYS day (without asking if he wanted me to do that). I wrote one final email and let him know that I was sorry (again), that I had refunded his $162, and that I would be happy to delete the content I had created for him if it wasn't a good reflection of the company. I did not hear back from that email.

You thought it was over didn't you? Well there's one more part to this story that proves my point that some clients simply don't have a clue. Almost a year later, I sent an email to the IWearYour-Shirt email list, which was made up mostly of fans, but some IWYS sponsors who had wanted updates from me via email. The email had something to do with an announcement of some media thing I was doing. And who responded? The owner of the beef jerky company. (Enter bafflement #3.) When I saw the "From" name, I knew exactly who it was. You rarely forget your negative experiences. I fully expected the email to be a continuation of where I left off a year prior and hadn't heard back.

Instead, the email read something along the lines of "Jason, I'm so proud of all your success! Keep doing great work!" WHAT!? I couldn't believe what I was reading. I checked the "From" name again in the email, as well as the email signature. Sure enough, it was the same person. I simply wrote back "Thank You" and went about the rest of my day. I couldn't believe it.

It was through this experience that I learned a few valuable lessons about dealing with bad clients. The first lesson was that I had to be explicit in what IWYS sponsors should expect, and more importantly, shouldn't expect from their IWYS days. This became a valuable exercise down the road for many potential IWYS buyers who would assume they'd get $5,000 in sales by spending $200 (no joke, that happened). The second lesson I learned was that you aren't going to make everyone happy, and that was okay. Up until then, all previous 161 IWYS sponsors had been extremely happy with the results of their t-shirt wearing advertising. That one bad experience was mostly out of my control. I did everything (and then some) to promote the company. When I realized that my ratio of happy to unhappy customers was 161:1, I stopped letting the negative situation bother me (though I'd be lying if I said it still didn't bother me just a tiny bit).

The last lesson I learned wouldn't become crystal clear until later, but I realized that *I could fire my bad clients*. If people came through and I got a bad feeling about them, or if they didn't seem like they'd be a good fit, I'd tell them "No thank you" for their business (in a very nice way, obviously). This rubbed some people the wrong way, but I always made sure to focus on the fact that I didn't think *I* could do a great job for them and that *I* wasn't a good fit to promote their business. I was perfectly happy to put the onus on me, if it meant I didn't have to potentially have a bad client.

Some bad clients won't be as noticeable as others. But the thing to make sure you think about, if you're in the client services business, is that there will always be more clients. You should make sure that the people and the companies you work with align with your core business values and goals. If they don't, it might be hard to say no to them, but it will be much worse in the long run if you don't rip the Band-Aid off early.

As obvious as it seems to make sure you take care of your customers and clients (aka the people who pay you), I see businesses put this on the back burner time and time again. Don't make that mistake. Take care of people, and they'll take care of you.

Accelir.com works with startup to F100 companies on employment branding, recruiting strategy & using HR technology for business success.

Chapter 16

LIFE AS AN ENTREPRENEUR: IT'S ALL ABOUT BALANCE

There's no handbook that tells you how to handle all the lifestyle changes that take place when you start building your own business. (Well, not until this chapter at least.) I had to learn about managing my time, being productive while working from home, keeping my health in check, and maintaining an overall sense of well-being the hard way. By sharing some of the major areas I struggled with while I was adjusting to life as an entrepreneur, I'm hoping you can avoid some of the mistakes I made and keep some level of balance in your life while you're pursuing your dream.

A HEALTHIER YOU IS A MORE CREATIVE YOU!

When I left my full-time job at the ATP and starting work from home, I found myself eating poorly, not getting much sleep, and spending way too much time on the couch. In short, I found it hard to actually focus and get work done.

When I turned 30 on May 15, 2012, I knew something had to change. My clothes weren't fitting well. I wasn't sleeping well. My workdays lasted forever. And I knew that my eating habits were far from healthy (just because you get chicken nuggets instead of a chicken sandwich at Chick-fil-A doesn't mean it's better for you!).

I hadn't stepped on a scale for quite some time because I didn't own one. I never needed it. I played basketball in college and stayed in great shape, although I didn't go to the gym much. After college (and two torn ACL ligaments in my knees later), I joined a gym and worked out regularly. All the years I was at a 9–5 job, I always took time to go to the gym during lunch or after work. I also had a fairly consistent eating schedule (small meals every 2–3 hours) and ate reasonably healthy (not much fast food).

When I started working from home, all of that changed. I worked long hours, often not eating anything or taking a sip of water for 6–8 hours at a time. I sat on my couch and typed away on my laptop all day long. I was consumed with working and never made time for food or exercise. When I worked a 9–5 job (and exercised often), I weighed around 210 pounds (reminder: I'm 6′5″ tall). Fast forward to a few days after my thirtieth birthday in May 2012, when—frustrated and wanting real data about where I was at with my weight—I went to Target. Shopping for a scale, for those who have never done it, is kind of like shopping for a present for your

Let's play sponsor a page tennis! Go to page 188. Wiggity Bang Games - WiggityBang.com weird uncle that you don't like much. It sucks. I knew I was out of shape but had no idea how much out of shape.

I brought the scale home, set it on the floor, and stepped on it. Fully expecting to have gained 10–15 pounds, I almost forgot how to breathe when the numbers read 2-6-5. Two hundred and sixty-five pounds! Are you kidding me? There had to be something wrong with the scale, right? I did what any logical person would do. I ran into my living room, picked up my dog Plaxico (who I knew weighed around 50 pounds), and carried him to the bathroom. If I stepped on the scale and it said anything higher than 315 pounds, I was going to return it to Target and demand a refund for the faulty product they sold me. With Plaxico in my arms (and my socks off, too), I stepped onto the scale again. The scale was going to spit out some crazy high number and obviously be defective. The numbers read 3-1-8. &%$#! Not only was the scale right, but I think even my dog had lost weight since he last went to the vet and got weighed (the jerk).

Two hundred and sixty-five pounds? I didn't feel like *all* my clothes fit terribly. I knew I wasn't sleeping well, but I figured that was just entrepreneurial stress. Then I took a second to think; I hadn't been to the gym in months. I couldn't remember the last day I went without eating some sort of sweet treat (read: half a package of chocolate chip cookies). And this neglect for my health and body had been compounding for years. Since the time I left the 9–5 world in 2007, I had gained 55 pounds. I was shocked. It was at that very moment that I said *enough*. I immediately went into my kitchen and threw away almost every piece of food in my pantry (because it was all processed, packaged, or just terrible— throwing away Kraft macaroni and cheese was heart wrenching). I opened my refrigerator and pulled out all the soda, sweat tea, and processed or fast food. And all while doing this, my wonderful Caroline stood by my side in support.

"If you're going to make changes, I'll be right there with you!" she said.

Starting on May 30, 2012, I embarked on a 90-day fitness and health challenge to change my lifestyle and my habits completely. I had tried a few diets here and there over the years (mostly around January 1 each year). I had also given P90X a shot in 2011. That was a joke. (For those who don't know, P90X is a workout series created by Tony Horton, who is possibly one of the most in-shape human beings alive. *"I hate it. But I love it!"*) This diet and fitness challenge was going to be different, so I decided to write about my plans and share it on my blog.

I didn't share exactly how out of shape I had gotten (because XL t-shirts hid it well, and I was truly embarrassed), but I wanted to keep myself accountable and let others join me if they felt the same way.

Over the course of the first two weeks, as I was sharing weekly updates about going back to the gym and making healthier meal choices, a previous IWearYourShirt sponsor reached out and had asked if I wanted help on my journey. That person was Tyler Ford (he owns page 178). He and his wife Mimi offered to be a part of my 90-day fitness challenge. Tyler and Mimi have a health and fitness coaching business, so my goal was right up their alley.

From the second I started talking to Tyler, I realized there was an opportunity to take this public fitness challenge and turn it into a business opportunity. The value I would bring to the table was the hard work and dedication to get in great shape and share my journey along the way. The return for Tyler was the exposure to an audience that would tune in to my weekly updates and final "transformation." We agreed that Tyler and Mimi would provide support

Interactive Events sparks interest via Educational Public Outreach. STEM combined with Arts, picks up STEAM, becoming TEAMS working together.

and come on as a sponsor of my journey. This is yet another example of recognizing what you bring to the table and thinking of a creative way to turn it into a money-making opportunity for you.

I have to admit, I was hesitant at first to make a business out of my fitness challenge, mostly because I was nervous I'd give up and have to give them their sponsorship money back. In actuality, their sponsorship of my fitness challenge was probably the most motivating factor of all to stick with it and work hard. I also consulted a personal trainer who, funny enough, my mom had met while sitting on a flight from Atlanta to NYC. That trainer was Fadi Malouf (Google him, he's an impressive man), and he would be integral for my mental challenges and nutrition planning.

Each week during the 90 days, I recorded a video of what I was doing, how I was feeling, and what steps I was taking to change my habits. Some of the steps were as simple as staring in the mirror in the morning and telling myself I could do it. Each day, with intention, I would look at myself and say out loud: "You will dominate this 90-day challenge and get back in shape." Other steps involved being more regimented in my grocery shopping (pro-tip: shop on the outer perimeter of the grocery store).

I filmed the second week's video and talked about the fact that I had a raging headache all week, most likely due to lack of sugar and excess sodium in my diet. Week after week, I shared exactly how I was feeling and the steps I was taking to get "back in shape" (I still hadn't told anyone exactly how out of shape I had gotten).

About 30 days into the challenge, I recorded a video talking about "goal shorts." These were a pair of shorts I had owned since college but hadn't been able to fit into for . . . who knows how long . . . Multiple people emailed me after I shared that video saying they, too, had "goal shorts, dresses, pants, jackets, etc." That was an amazing feeling.

Cardd.com

With each passing week of the challenge, I tried to be more intentional with my daily routine when it came to eating, drinking water, and avoiding trouble ($1 slices of pizza on Thursdays at a local pizza place were always trouble). On day 60, I stepped on the scale and saw 2-3-5. I had successfully lost 30 pounds and was inspired, sleeping better, and feeling all-around more productive. It was like I had been exercising my brain and shedding excess weight from it as well. During the final 30 days, I kicked my challenge into high gear. Because I had way more energy each morning, I started waking up earlier and earlier. Some mornings, I actually felt like going to the gym early (which I was previously allergic to). Other days, I hopped in the pool for 20 minutes (wearing my bathing suit that actually fit without dreaded muffin-tops [ugh, those suck]). My eating routine became second nature. And while doing all of this stuff for my health and fitness, I noticed my work seemed to get done faster as well. No longer was I up until 2:00 in the morning editing IWYS videos; I was actually going to sleep around midnight each night.

As I spent more time organizing my eating and workout schedules, I also became more focused on certain work I was doing. Getting in better shape had actually helped me become more productive, and that was completely a by-product.

I wasn't nervous at all going into the last week of the 90-day challenge. Instead, I was motivated and excited. I knew I had already lost a good amount of weight. I knew my clothes were fitting better. And I knew that when I looked in the mirror I was so much happier with what I saw. I booked a photography session with my good friend Laura Evans, who always did my professional photography work for IWearYourShirt and BuyMyLastName. From the beginning, I had dreams of taking these awesome "after" photos and comparing them to my less-than-amazing "before" photos. Before I left the house to drive to Laura's studio, I stepped on the scale. I don't think I had weighed myself a week or two prior to that day. The numbers read 2-2-1. I had successfully lost 44 pounds! The photos that Laura ended up taking were exactly what I had hoped for. It wasn't until I put my "after" photos side-by-side with my "before" photos that I could see just how terribly out of shape I had gotten.

Not only had I knocked my 90-day challenge out of the park and gotten into the best shape of my life, I had also created new habits and a completely new lifestyle for myself. I was healthier. I was happier. I had awesome before and after photos. And I had become immensely more productive in multiple aspects of my life.

I'm sharing all of this with you because I experienced firsthand the danger in being an entrepreneur and becoming consumed with building your business. The danger is that you simply forget to take care of yourself. From the beginning, make sure you devote the time you need for your health. Sure, I managed to turn the unfortunate decline in my health into a positive thing through the 90-day challenge, but it wasn't easy and I wouldn't recommend it. It's a much better idea to keep an eye on your balance from the beginning, not just for your health, but for your productivity and your happiness, too.

PRODUCTIVITY AND HAPPINESS

In 2012, before I made the realization that I had let my health deteriorate (and subsequently, my happiness and productivity), I had little energy to respond to inquiries from prospective IWearYour-Shirt buyers. Some of them were big organizations, wanting to do something unique with IWYS, but they were looking to me to brainstorm and offer ideas. In the past, I could crank these ideas

ShowTees.com is all about the glittery world of ShowBiz. Every shirt we make tells a unique story from real life inspiration to fantasy.

out in no time at all. It never felt like work, and I looked forward to doing it. Because I hadn't taken care of my body (and mind), this became something of a burden for me. I'd see these emails hit my inbox, sometimes daily, and the effort it felt like it would take to respond was equivalent to lifting a giant anvil from a Wile E Coyote cartoon. These inquiry emails went from exciting opportunities to burdensome negativity. Some days, I treated my email inbox like a horrible skin rash. I'd stare at it blankly, but I did nothing to fix it. I didn't have any processes in place for my life or business, and both had suffered the consequences. I won't name names, but I let an opportunity for IWYS to work with a Fortune 100 company slip through my fingers because writing a creative email back to them felt like excruciating work. That may sound ridiculous, but because I had gotten to a point where I had no physical or creative energy, those opportunities didn't bring me happiness anymore. They just felt like work. But by making changes to take care of my health, I finally felt productive again. Feeling more productive brought back my creativity, and I was able to juggle the various opportunities and inquiries that were pouring in on a daily basis. Once I regained my handle on that, my overall sense of happiness improved as well.

WHERE TO START WITH PRODUCTIVITY? A SCHEDULE!

When you own your own business or work from home, the allure of setting your own schedule is very exciting. You think about your ability to sleep in, stay in your Teenage Mutant Ninja Turtle footie pajamas all day, and never have to schedule another meeting before 11:00 a.m. But, truth be told, it can also be wildly distracting. When you work in a traditional office setting, you have structure, certain hours you work, and not too many distractions. Everyone knows

Barbara Buchana bought lucky page #100. Maybe you can Google her name? That could be fun!

it's a place of work and that they're supposed to be doing their jobs. When you're your own boss, you let yourself slack on getting things done, you make excuses, and you often don't shower for days (well, maybe that's just me.) In order to avoid the work-from-home productivity trap, I've found that having a loose schedule will actually make you more productive (and happier in the long run).

Before I started IWearYourShirt, I worked from home for about a year. The first few weeks were glorious! I slept in every single day. All of my calls were scheduled in the afternoons. I could go run errands (read: go to the beach for an hour with my dog) whenever I wanted. I was the king of the world! About a month in, I started missing deadlines. Then I missed a few phone calls due to scheduling the times wrong. Then I couldn't seem to get a handle on my to-do lists. I really didn't have that much work to do, but for some reason, none of it was getting done.

I realized that not having a simple schedule was killing my productivity. Humans, like other animals, are creatures of habit. Our brains are efficient organs, and as we repeat tasks, they become much more second nature. This goes for good habits and bad habits. The more I started my workday at random times, the less I was ever able to get done in the morning. Even if I got up earlier here and there, my brain just wasn't prepared to work. The more often I took random breaks throughout the day to goof off, the less able I was to focus on my work during the middle of the day. So right there, I had lost virtually all morning and afternoon productivity because I had no structure. That's a lot of time to lose.

So what I started doing was setting loose "office hours" for myself. My workday was never going to start later than 10:00 a.m., and if I had *errands* to run, I would only do them during my lunchtime or between noon and 2:00 p.m. I also told myself that I would close my laptop at 6:00 p.m. to make dinner, exercise, or hang out with friends and family. Now, did I stick to these hours like you'd have to at a corporate job? No. But, it gave me a foundation and really helped me start to streamline my workdays. In no time, I was getting work done, knocking out to-do lists, and keeping one day's tasks from spilling over to the next.

GOING ANALOG WITH MY TO-DO LISTS

In 2012, there was a lot going on with IWearYourShirt. Along with four other Shirt Wearers, there was an Operations Manager (Heather), a Client Relations Manager (Caroline, my girlfriend), and a Super Intern Extraordinaire (Burton aka "Burtle"). This tiny t-shirt idea had grown immensely, and I was feeling the weight of it on a day-to-day basis. That weight wasn't just the financial burden; it was also my daily to-do list burden.

I had always been good at managing my to-do lists, especially after being more focused while checking email, having a more scheduled workday, and having people help take work off my plate (Heather, Caroline, and Burtle). By 2012, we had learned a lot and were trying shared to-do list applications. These shared to-do lists would show everybody what everyone else was working on, so there was group accountability and some semblance of daily processes for "t-shirt wearing." One of these applications that worked really well was called TeuxDeux (clever huh?). TeuxDeux was well designed and worked beautifully. You'd enter your to-do items, in list form, for each day of the week. If you didn't accomplish your to-dos for the current day, they would automatically spill over into the next day. It was great . . . in the beginning. But then I noticed I kept adding items each day but not completing all of the previous ones, and my list just got bigger and bigger.

One day while working on my to-do list, an item involved posting something on Facebook. As I clicked out of the to-do list browser tab to Facebook, I immediately completed my task. But then I clicked the "Home" button on Facebook. I was already on Facebook, so I figured I may as well read some recent status updates from friends. Oh, and then someone commented on a photo I had posted earlier, so I had to click that notification to read the comment and respond with something witty. Then, someone started a Facebook chat with me. Before I knew it, I had spent an hour on Facebook and completely ignored the rest of my to-do items. TeuxDeux was a wonderful product, but because my to-dos were always going to come from another browser window, this inefficiency was bound to happen again.

A friend recently attended a conference and heard a talk called "Get Shit Done." Because I was probably preoccupied checking Facebook while he was telling me about it, I don't recall every detail, but the gist was to take your to-do list items and physically write them down in a notebook. The are two reasons for doing this:

1. By writing down your to-do list, you can do a brain dump. You won't get distracted by any pop-up notifications like you would on your computer. Could you imagine if your notebook had some sort of page-pop-up thing—like another page just randomly slid in front of the page you were writing on? That would suck. Really puts into perspective how disruptive notifications can be, huh?

2. Physically crossing out to-do items on your list is therapeutic. This is 100% true for me. Each time I can draw a big black

(or red if it's one of *those* days) line through a to-do item, I feel great. Yeah, it's not "I just won the lottery" great, but it's definitely more satisfying that checking a box online or deleting some text on a screen.

When I was first adopting this analog strategy to my to-do lists, I would force myself to write out my to-dos first thing every day. I'd even write mundane things like "make coffee" and "eat lunch." It felt silly at first, but now I'm a to-do list champion. I tear through my to-dos with a reckless abandon. Don't get in the way of my notebook to-do pages or you might lose an eye! (I'm just kidding, you won't lose an eye . . . *maybe*.)

AVOIDING BURNOUT

While trying to maximize your productivity is great, the goal is not to work yourself to the bone; the goal is balance. Work/life balance is not something you ever stop working on, but it is something you can definitely get better at. Take it from someone who worked 882 straight days without a full day off. You can quickly alienate a lot of people in your life if you aren't careful. Oh, and you can also burn out.

Early on, people told me, "Jason, wearing t-shirts 365 days a year is a lot. You should really think about taking time off so you don't burn out." Psshhhh! That's just the talk of weak people who can't work as hard as me.

NOPE!

Those people were 100% right, probably because they had some similar life experience to go on. When I worked 882 days straight, every day consisted of 14–16 hours of work.

From January 1, 2009, to May 31, 2011, I didn't take a single day off. Not on Christmas. Not on Thanksgiving (some of you may remember playing board games with my family and me on Ustream). Especially not on New Year's Eve or New Year's Day when the new IWearYourShirt sponsor calendar rolled out. I spent one New Year's Eve on my computer from 9:00–11:59 p.m., stepped away for a minute to kiss my girlfriend and drink champagne, and then sat back down for another three hours. Years of that kind of dedication with zero breaks will wear on you, no matter who you are.

This brings up another point about setting your schedule and avoiding burnout. When you're ready to end your workday, make sure you **actually end your workday**. Close your laptop, and don't look at it again until the next day. You are going to feel like you're missing out on opportunities and time you could be working, but it's so worth it in the long run to relax and let your mind and body recharge. This is a lesson that took me years to learn, and believe me when I say I'm a better person now because of it. There's no telling how much more creative I could have been, or what other whacky business ideas I might have come up with over the years had I given my brain a break here and there early on. No matter what business or entrepreneurial adventure you plan to embark on, do yourself a favor and schedule time off. You may feel like you HAVE to be checking email and working, but trust, *trust*, trust me, you'll be just fine. Burning out is much more detrimental in the long haul than having someone not get an email response for two days.

THERE WILL ALWAYS BE MORE EMAIL

There's this funny thing about email. It simply just keeps coming. Whether it's inbound leads, client follow-ups, friends and family stuff, or the 249 newsletters you're subscribed to. Whatever it is, your inbox is always going to be a somewhat noisy and uncontrolled space.

Being productive with email is tough; I'm not going to sugarcoat it. One of the ways I've changed the way I handle email came from reading Tim Ferriss' *The 4-Hour Work Week*. (If you haven't read Tim's book, I'd highly recommend it, not only for his tips about being more productive with email but also as an all-around great resource and inspiration for entrepreneurs.) Tim talks about his more drastic approach to handling email. He only answers email twice a day. Yep. I remember reading that and being shocked. Twice a day? I'm lucky if I check my email less than twice a MINUTE, let alone an hour, or, haha, a day!

What Tim says he does is set two times a day where he sits down with his email and does nothing else. At 10:00 a.m. and 4:00 p.m., he closes all other applications on his computer, sets his phone in another room, and focuses only on email. This makes him completely focus on email, with no distractions. When I read this, it made sense. That being said, I knew I couldn't go cold turkey on my current email habits and do what Tim does. Instead, I picked up one simple habit from what Tim does: I only check email when I am checking email. Whether I'm checking email after being away from my computer for a few hours or after I finished some other task and hop into my inbox, I make a concerted effort to only focus on emails. It's so easy to pop back and forth between email, Facebook, and funny cat videos on YouTube. But when I started to adopt this one small tip from Tim, I noticed my email consumption and output increase dramatically.

I used to find it daunting when 50 unread emails were waiting for me, but not anymore. Now, it feels like any other achievable task and I get it done.

Whether you want to get as crazy with your email checking schedule as Tim Ferriss, or you want to adopt a strategy somewhere closer to what I do, be deliberate about it. Give yourself time to get used to a new way of checking email, and be in the moment with email. (Not like a romantic moment though. That would be weird.)

THREE EMAIL TOOLS I USE DAILY (GMAIL ONLY)

I quickly want to share three email tools I use that help for keeping track of contact information and following up on pitches or simple reminders.

1. **Evercontact.com:** A simple to use service that you plug your Gmail account into and it will scour through old emails and build a contact list for you based on email signatures. The cool thing about Evercontact is that they have a "flashback" service that goes back as far as five years (it may even go further). As of writing this book, I'm proud to announce that I had the most emails they'd ever encountered in a five-year flashback: 220,000. Not sure if I should be proud or petrified of that.

2. **Followup.cc:** A super simple and fantastic service that will revolutionize the way you follow up with pitch emails or set reminders in your inbox. When I was pitching companies I didn't know about buying page sponsorships in this book, I added "7days@followup.cc" to the Bcc of my email pitches. What this does is set an automatic email reminder with Followup.cc and it will send an email to remind me in 7 days. The cool thing is that you can set the "7 days" to whatever

The people you surround yourself with are integral to your success. Spend time with people who challenge you to grow & develop. @jessiet09

times you want: 30 minutes, 2 hours, 2 months, virtually any amount of time. And the best part is that Followup.cc is completely free. I swear by it and use it all the time.

3. **Rapportive.com:** My good friend Clay Hebert turned me on to Rapportive, and it's a really smart extension for Gmail. Once you install it (100% free), it will include a sidebar in Gmail that shows you the full contact information for the person you're currently emailing with. So, if Clay sent me an email, when I open it, I see a photo of Clay in the sidebar, along with links to his Facebook, Twitter, and LinkedIn accounts, a short bio for him, and whatever other information Rapportive can find about him quickly. It's a great tool for Gmail users.

The takeaway here is to simply be smart and consistent about how you attack the email monster, and you can easily loosen the death grip it has on your work/life balance.

KNOW WHEN (AND WHEN NOT) TO SACRIFICE

A few years ago, I missed out on a friend's wedding because I had accepted a consulting gig for a company that randomly emailed me. To be fair, I *did* accept the consulting gig long before I found out about my friend's wedding. But the problem here is that I didn't actually want to do the consulting gig. The company wasn't one that I genuinely cared about (no offense to them; they were great people), but I thought I needed the money. And I'll be honest; the money was pretty damn good.

When I got my friend's letter in the mail, I knew what it was. I opened it, excited to read his and his future wife's announcement and find out when the wedding would be. When I saw the date on the hand-scripted card, my heart dropped. It was a date I knew I had already booked on my calendar.

I remember it clear as day: I stood in my kitchen with the letter in my hand as the Florida sun poured in through the kitchen windows. I grabbed my phone and checked my calendar just to make sure (although I already knew). (Sure enough, it was the same date.) I RSVPed "No" and put the invitation back in the self-addressed envelope that had come in the announcement letter. Just like that, I had picked a consulting gig over a friend's wedding.

As the wedding got closer, I felt awful. I had talked to my friend a few months after sending the RSVP and told him I had a "huge business opportunity I couldn't pass up." You want to know the unfortunate thing? While the consulting gig went well and they were happy with my work, all I could think about was how it wasn't more important that my friend's wedding.

The hardest part was that I didn't even ask the business if we could reschedule the consulting meeting for another time. I was just so caught up in thinking I had to take the opportunity because it paid well and because "consulting" is such a cool thing to do as an entrepreneur (or small business owner).

When the consulting gig was over, I felt terrible. I had picked doing work for a random company instead of spending cherished time with a friend. I had a pit in my stomach for weeks (especially after the wedding photos went up on Facebook).

I've been fortunate to still stay close with this friend, even though I didn't attend one of the most important moments he and his wife will ever share. It was the slap in the face that I needed. I never put business before friendships anymore, no matter how big the opportunity is.

WooThemes is a market leader providing a platform to extend standard WordPress-powered websites via a range of innovative themes and plugins

When you're an entrepreneur, in many ways YOU are your business. If you don't take care of yourself, the business can suffer. Email, scheduling your days, working out . . . it may all seem insignificant, but I promise these are things that can impact your bottom line more than you might think. Hopefully, now you can take away a few strategies to best manage and balance these areas of your life.

Awesome Balance-Finder 3000 Illustration
by Caroline Winegeart – *www.MadeVibrant.com*

Hundred10: all of our pixels are certified cruelty-free.

SECTION 3: WE'VE LAID THE FOUNDATION; NOW LET'S ACT

Marketing, social media, product launches, oh my! While the last section was more about getting the fundamentals of your business idea in place, the next few chapters are focused on helping you price and sell your products and/or services. Remember, no one has the "Midas Touch" when it comes to business or marketing. Iteration, trial and error, and just putting your stuff out in the world is the most important part.

millionairemobile.com wants you to be a part of our HUGE vehicle advertising collage. A unique, fun, and cost effective way to advertise.

Chapter 17

HOW TO CATCH A UNICORN NAMED "MARKETING"

My first foray into marketing came via Seth Godin's book *The Purple Cow*. If you haven't read the book, I'll sum it up very quickly for you: Cows are predominantly white and black. Being a purple cow would be unique and make you stand out from the rest. Therefore, being a purple cow is marketing. There's obviously *much* more to Seth's book, but after reading it, a light bulb went on.

It seems so simple, but we see the success of others in our relative industries and want to emulate them. Instead, we should strive to stand out from them. This was my entire thought process when starting IWearYourShirt, BuyMyLastName, and even SponsorMy-Book. Millions of people were already on Facebook and Twitter, but none of them were leveraging their following to make money by wearing t-shirts and creating content. Tons of people have had unfortunate family situations that have left them with a last name they didn't want, but none of them decided to auction it off. There

Tantrums. Stalling. Disrespect. AARGH! TiredOfYelling.com's MP3 download shows you how to raise amazing kids without attending a workshop.

are hundreds—maybe thousands—of authors writing books every day, but they're either making no money when they self-publish or making no money when they sign with big book publishers. I was determined to be different.

Great marketing doesn't have to be expensive and doesn't require a college degree. What great marketing takes is thinking outside the box and doing things differently. At times, this can feel like you're chasing the tail of a unicorn. Each strand of the hair on that tail is a different type of marketing. Some marketing campaigns can go on forever and don't even look like marketing. Some campaigns have a short time to live, which is perfectly okay. Some marketing is controlled. Some is uncontrolled. There's probably an entire book I could write on marketing (and might), but let's start with those ideas first.

MARKETING THAT DOESN'T LOOK LIKE MARKETING (BUT IS MARKETING)

The lifespan of any type of marketing campaign (print, TV, social, etc.) is incredibly hard to predict. But sometimes you can use the same marketing campaign over and over, and it will always work. Zappos is a perfect example of a company doing marketing that doesn't look like marketing.

Zappos' free overnight shipping and amazing customer service has been its best form of marketing since day one. Ask anyone who's ever ordered anything from Zappos.com, and they'll tell you they had a great experience. If they didn't, that person is probably some sort of under-the-bridge-dwelling troll-creature who hates

MARKETING: ANYTHING THAT IS MEANT TO GIVE YOUR COMPANY AN EDGE OVER THE COMPETITION.

ManMade: It's What's Underneath That Counts... Form fitting, smooth feeling, fully tucked undershirts for the metro man at manmadestore.com.

butterflies and sunny days. (No offense to all my fans that are trolls who live under bridges! Love you guys!)

A few years ago, I ordered a pair of running shoes from Zappos and spent $10 more than I would had I ordered them from Eastbay, another online shoe store that carries epically large shoes for people who have giant feet like me (size 16). You know what they say about big feet . . . Eh, eh? (sorry). I ordered a pair of *super* awesome red Nike Free running shoes at 2:00 p.m. on a Tuesday, and they arrived at my door at 11:00 a.m. the next day. That's well worth the extra $10, but that wasn't the only bonus with this order.

About a month into owning and wearing the running shoes often (full disclosure: I never ran in them), they started to make a weird squeaking sound when I walked. It was almost as annoying as the sound you hear when someone's pulls the opening of a balloon sideways and it goes *weeeeeeeeeeeep* (almost that annoying, not quite). I knew I had worn the shoes a bunch and that most companies probably wouldn't have done anything about it. I decided *"what the heck?"* and hopped online to chat with a Zappos customer service person just in case. I was fully prepared for them to say *"sorry, not our problem."* But they—of course—did not. I explained the situation, and along with being super cheery and happy, the customer service representative told me they'd ship a brand new pair to me, free of charge, and I could send the other pair back so they could inspect them.

The new pair arrived the next day with a return label already in the box for my squeaky pair. My new pair of running shoes didn't squeak and never got run in (at least I'm consistent!). That type of service is marketing in itself, because here you are, reading about it in my book. And I'm sure you've either had your own great experience with Zappos and shared it or you have a friend who's had one.

Download this awesome app: www.bit.ly/thisawesomeapp

I challenge you to think about what you can do with your existing or new business that could be ongoing marketing for you. Sometimes it's nothing crazy; it's just amazing customer service. There's absolutely nothing wrong with that. No one ever stopped buying products from a company because "the customer service was just too damn amazing."

ONE-TIME MARKETING EXPLOSION (POW!)

Sometimes your marketing plan can only work well once. And that's totally okay!

Grasshopper.com launched its VOIP (Voice Over Internet Protocol, or more simply: telephone on the Internet) service in May of 2009 by doing something totally out of the box. The company made a list of 5,000 influential people, which included celebrities, social media people, press folks, politicians, and more, and then mailed each individual person five chocolate covered grasshoppers (yuck!). Also in the package with the decadent grasshoppers was a small piece of paper with the URL to a really cool launch video Grasshopper spent a lot of time and money on.

Grasshopper.com had no clue if people would find receiving these sugar-covered-insects disgusting or if find it interesting and talk about it. The company also spent a sizable amount of cash on this idea ($60,000+) and had no guarantee that it would work. But, as people started to receive these gross, chocolate-covered insect gifts, they definitely had to talk about them. Media folks ate the grasshoppers during TV segments. Prominent Twitter users (like Guy Kawasaki, Kevin Rose, and Jason Calacanis) tweeted photos of themselves eating the grasshoppers or just holding the package (which clearly showed the Grasshopper.com logo and video URL).

"Brands are built (not created)" ... What the hell's that mean? Find out more at saywhat.com.

For two months, Grasshopper's marketing campaign worked like a chocolate covered charm. The company had amassed nearly 200,000 views on their launch video and over 50,000 website visits, plus over 170 blog posts or news articles were written about Grasshopper. It was a huge success and exactly the explosive launch hoped for, because let's face it: Internet telephones are not that exciting.

Shortly thereafter, the buzz died down and the web traffic leveled out on the Grasshopper.com website. But the company had accomplished its goal. I'm certain that sending a bunch more people chocolate covered grasshoppers (still yuck) today wouldn't do much good. Now, if the company sent live grasshoppers . . . That'd be an entirely different story.

What you need to remember is that marketing is a continual effort and is only as good as the product or service you are selling. You can have the most amazing marketing idea in the world, but if your products suck a unicorn's horn, you'll never see great results. Grasshopper.com was using this one-time explosive marketing campaign to re-launch its company. Learning from previous mistakes, the company had greatly improved its VOIP product (and rebranded the company). This was the perfect campaign and well worth the money spent on it. [I want to know if you check out Grasshopper.com after reading this story! Shoot me an email if you do: *jason@sponsormybook.com*]

(ONTROLLED VS. UN(ONTROLLED MARKETING

Marketing comes in all shapes and sizes, but over the course of marketing my own businesses, I've identified these two distinct groups into which all initiatives fit.

CONTROLLED MARKETING

Controlled marketing is made up of campaigns you set up and expect clear results from. Examples are email marketing, most direct mail marketing (unless you send grasshoppers), and pay-per-click advertising. Typically, controlled marketing has a finite reach, which is perfectly okay.

Mike Faith, the CEO of Headsets.com (you may remember them from my last name in 2013) is a brilliant marketer (and not just because he bought my last name). Mike and his marketing team do a good bit of well-executed controlled marketing. They effectively use banner ads and direct mailers to reach their audience and generate sales. They've become incredibly efficient at doing controlled marketing and know how much of a return they can expect with their standard discounts and offers to their existing (or potential) customers. They've identified strategies that work in a somewhat predictable way so they can throttle those initiatives up or down, depending on their desired results.

What controlled marketing are you thinking about doing? If you've never done direct mail, find a friend who has and learn from them. If you're thinking about doing Facebook advertising (a very solid example of controlled marketing), make sure you work with someone who has experience, as there are a ton of variables involved. And remember: your controlled marketing campaign doesn't have to last forever. It can be a one-time thing, and there's nothing wrong with that.

UNCONTROLLED MARKETING (COME BACK HERE, UNICORN!)

Uncontrolled marketing can come in many forms, but it typically comes from a plan or strategy with results you can't predict, control, or expect. Examples are word of mouth marketing and big

// FROM JASON: Write down the next word that comes to your mind
_____. (Now email a photo of this to me!)

media mentions. These types of marketing efforts often have the potential for the largest ROI but can be hit or miss. When I launched IWearYourShirt and started emailing my contacts and engaging with people on Twitter, this was controlled marketing. My messages could only go so far, and the results were somewhat minimal. When I purchased the advertisement in Peter Shankman's HARO (that text ad I bought in 2008), I was dabbling in uncontrolled marketing.

Here's a perfect example. In 2011, then 96-year-old Bill Sleeper rocked the retirement community world with his use of technology and social media. Mr. Sleeper was a resident of Merrill Gardens, a Senior Care Community with multiple locations around the country. Along with using social media and creating content to reach younger demographics, such as those that usually make the decisions to move their older family members into retirement communities, Merrill Gardens found a superstar in their Seattle, Washington, retirement community location in Bill Sleeper. Bill, from all outside appearances, does not look like a marketing or technology guru. However, Bill carries an iPhone and a laptop with him wherever he goes, and he has been quoted saying "If you have a finger, you're all set." (If anyone knows any 90 year olds that are social media or tech savvy, please send them my way!)

Merrill Gardens had done a solid job of marketing their retirement community through social media, which, at the time, not many other retirement communities did. One day, an employee stumbled upon Mr. Sleeper helping a fellow resident with something on the computer. After further inspection, the employee found out that Mr. Sleeper was not only setting up a WiFi network (which I don't even know how to do), but was also educating his fellow resident on how to use social media to stay in touch with his family.

// FROM JASON: Did you write down that word from the last page and email it to me yet? My email address is jason@sponsormybook.com.

When the PR and marketing team at Merrill Gardens caught wind of Mr. Sleeper's technological efforts, they put him at the forefront of all the marketing they were doing.

They wrote blog posts highlighting Mr. Sleeper's technology expertise—blog posts that I'm sure he checked for proper social media optimization. They shared photos of him on his iPhone. Those photos weren't selfies, but I'm willing to bet Mr. Sleeper had a few of those in his photo library. They pitched local media with stories of a senior citizen who was tech savvy and effectively using social media. And the press absolutely loved it. Merrill Gardens was written up by GeekWire, Forbes, and nearly every media outlet in Seattle. Mr. Sleeper even attended a Social Media Club event in 2011, holding his iPhone above his head like a trophy as he was helped through the event with the aid of his walker. I wouldn't be surprised if Mr. Sleeper created an iPhone app that could communicate with a walker to see if it needs maintenance. Merrill Gardens had previously only focused on controlled marketing and had great success with it. When they found Mr. Sleeper, uncontrolled marketing fell right into their lap.

The smart thing that Merrill Gardens did was to leverage this story and share it with the world. I'm sure they'd pitched stories to local media before about social media—with little response. But with Mr. Sleeper, they had a story that was impossible to ignore, and it got more attention than any other previous marketing efforts.

(CONTROLLED + UNCONTROLLED MARKETING (THE UNITAUR)

Think of this as the offspring of a Unicorn and a Minotaur: a Unitaur, if you will. This is when you've laid the groundwork with controlled marketing and one of your marketing efforts takes off like an uncontrollable, flying, half-horse-half-man creature.

At Madison Glass Co. we pour our passion for typography and sign painting techniques into simple, quality, hand painted glassware.

Epic Unitaur illustration by Nick Jarvis – *www.nckjrvs.com*

Old Spice (which, fun fact, has been around since 1934) introduced body wash for men in 2003. They were one of the first companies to have body wash but certainly not the last.

As body wash sales increased and bar soap decreased, other brands started creating body wash: Dial, Irish Spring, Nivea, and plenty more. By 2009, every soap company for men had a body wash. And in 2010, Dove had announced that its Men+Care body wash was going to be featured in a Super Bowl commercial. Old Spice found itself worried about protecting its share of the *keep ALL the manly men clean* category (yes, I made that up).

Old Spice had done plenty of controlled marketing up to this point. All the standard things a men's grooming product would do. But they knew they had to do something different to stand out. They partnered with the acclaimed advertising agency Wieden+Kennedy to create "The Man Your Man Could Smell Like" YouTube video campaign. In the video, Isaiah Mustafa, a very handsome ex-NFL player, stood in a bathroom wearing only a towel and holding a bottle of Old Spice body wash. With his chiseled physique and recognizable deep voice, Isaiah spoke directly to the viewer with clever and unusual copy written by the creators of the campaign.

Old Spice marketed the video through paid ads, promoted tweets on Twitter, sponsored posts on Facebook, etc. With its charming script and one-take-video wonderment, it went on to amass several million views on YouTube.

Old Spice found itself with a great video, a well-received character, and some decent fanfare on social media. Then Old Spice took a gamble and did something they had no clue would take off like it did (uncontrolled marketing! Unitaur! Ah!).

Isaiah Mustafa put the towel back around his waist, hopped back in front of the shower stall in the bathroom, grabbed his bottle of Old Spice body wash, and proceeded to do something unheard of. In real time, Old Spice filmed and shared YouTube videos where "the Old Spice man" would answer questions from fans that mentioned Old Spice on Twitter, Facebook, YouTube, Reddit, Yahoo Answers, and Digg. The "Response" video campaign was born. Old

Did you know the emergency telephone number in Austria is 122 (not 911)? #knowledge

Spice used its YouTube channel to share the video responses to the millions of viewers that were already there. The comapny started by creating response videos to people who had online influence, like Ellen DeGeneres, Perez Hilton, and Kevin Rose. Then it created video responses where Isaiah talked to average Joes. Within 72 hours, there were 185 video responses, 70% of them to non-celebrities. The views poured in! In the first day, Old Spice's videos had been seen by almost 6,000,000 people. On day two, Old Spice had 8 of the top 11 most popular videos on YouTube. By day three, the campaign had over 20,000,000 views. And after the first week, over 40,000,000 viewers had looked at Isaiah Mustafa's washboard abs. Old Spice could never have imagined the success of its "response" video marketing campaign. The Old Spice Twitter following was up 2,700%, Facebook fans shot up 800%, the Old Spice YouTube account became the #1 all-time most viewed branded channel, and sales of the body wash rose 125% from the previous year. Old Spice went on to become the #1 selling body wash and has stayed at or near the top since then. This is most likely due to upping the ante on the weirdness of advertising and marketing. But hey, who am I to point fingers? I live for weird and unconventional!

Old Spice was able to create this controlled + uncontrolled (Unitaur) marketing campaign because the company was willing to take a risk and directly engage with the fan base it had built from its first marketing efforts. While I completely realize that we normal business owners don't have the big budget of a company like Old Spice, we certainly have the ability to think outside the box and try unconventional (or never tried before) marketing efforts if we want to generate unexpected returns.

Let's bring Headsets.com back into the picture for a moment. This company also applies uncontrolled marketing to its controlled

DuckGPS: Grow. Play. Share. Set your Duck on a worldwide adventure and follow it every step of the way. DuckGPS.com.

marketing. Instead of just sending standard direct mailers that say something like, "We're Headsets.com, buy our newest headset!", the mailers sometimes feature fun and interesting offers. One a few years ago was a sealed envelope that had a message on the outside stating "This offer excludes Apple, Boeing, and Whole Foods employees!" This mailer went to everyone, including customers that the company knew worked for Apple, Boeing, and Whole Foods. Imagine receiving that piece of mail. You'd be interested to know why Headsets.com would be excluding those companies, right?

Well, it worked in two ways. First, Headsets.com received phone calls from people who worked for Apple, Boeing, and Whole Foods, asking why they couldn't take advantage of the offer they received in the mail. The Headsets.com customer service reps would politely tell them they had nothing against them, it was just an offer that excluded them. Then, and this is where Mike Faith and his team are genius marketers, they'd offer the Apple, Boeing, and Whole Foods people a better deal than was in the mailer. Smart, right? Of course, they took the better deal. The other way that this exclusivity offer worked for Headsets.com was that other customers **called** in asking why Headsets.com would exclude the offer from Apple, Boeing, and Whole Foods employees? Did you notice the word I put in bold? Headsets.com *doubled* their inbound call volume by sending a mailer that excluded three big companies.

Mike and his team figured the offer would do well but were shocked when this experiment doubled the normal response rate. You don't have to be Old Spice to pull off something unique and attention grabbing.

Whether you're doing controlled, uncontrolled, or Unitar marketing, you should always be thinking about marketing campaigns. If they fail miserably, that's fine. What can you learn from your mistakes and then implement into the next campaign to make it better? Don't be afraid to takes risks with your marketing, and budget for those risks to fail (or bring zero returns). Not all marketing has a directly measurable ROI, and I'm walking and talking proof of that.

As with any marketing effort, you should make sure you have a foundation in place first. Is your product ready to go to market? If you're doing email marketing (which you better be, or I'll punch you in the jejunum [semi-pro reference, anyone?]), are you ready to capture information if you have an influx of customers? Oh, and is your plan for handling customer service in place? Think of marketing like preparing for running a marathon. You wouldn't just go out tomorrow and try to run 26.1 miles with no previous training, running shoes, or mental preparation (how people run marathons is beyond me). The majority of us would crash and burn after the first few miles and then be unable to get off the couch for a month. Make sure to take care of the foundational stuff (great product, customer service, etc.) and be as prepared as possible for your next marketing campaign.

Chapter 18

SOCIAL MEDIA: THE GOOD, THE BAD, THE UGLY

Social media is like a giant house party that's been going on for years. Back in 2006, the party was relatively small. Facebook was only two years old and just starting to go from college-only to an open platform that anyone with an email address could join. Twitter had just launched, and most people didn't know what to think of it (or say on it besides "I just showered"). YouTube was only a year old and still basking in the glory of the "Lazy Sunday" video.

At this social media house party, you felt like you could walk around and mingle with anyone. When you sent a tweet or updated a Facebook status, people actually saw it and responded. There certainly weren't many brands pitching their products. Oh, and there definitely weren't any social media experts, mavens, ninjas, whatever (please people, stop calling yourself these things). Social media was an incredibly effective way to communicate with people, and you were almost guaranteed a response because there were relatively few people on these networks.

Long before I started IWearYourShirt, I attended South By Southwest SXSW in 2007 with my design company co-founder Dennis from Thought & Theory. This was our first time attending SXSW, and we had only decided to go because we had landed a big retainer client the month before. We were excited at the opportunity to attend SXSW, to see downtown Austin, Texas, and to learn as much as we could about what was going on in our respective industries (design for Dennis, and marketing for me).

I attended a panel that was geared toward using Twitter for your companies. It was during that panel that I pulled my iPhone out of my pocket and signed up for a Twitter account (hello @ thejasonsadler, Twitter account # 696,013). I listened to the panel members talk about hash tags, which were simply words after a "#" symbol (e.g., #CreativityForSale). They talked about how they were starting conversations with complete strangers by using a popular hash tag and asking questions.

Being the curious extrovert I was (and still am), one of my first tweets was "Does anyone want to meet up at #SXSW?" Within seconds, I had people at SXSW replying that they'd love to meet at a certain lounge or at a party later that day. At the time, I was less-than-nobody, but Twitter was just that small and people were actually listening and engaging. Funny enough, someone in the same room a few seats to my right saw my tweet and tweeted back at me.

Nowadays when you send a tweet, you'll be lucky if you get a response, let alone meet up with new people at crowded events where everyone is tweeting and haphazardly using hash tags. #end-ofparagraph #youarereadingmybook #creativityforsale #book

When I got more active on Twitter, Facebook, and YouTube in 2008, there were definitely a lot more users, but the party was

30DayThis30DayThat.com is a website detailing life one #30daychallenge at a time. What's your 30 day challenge? Check us out!

still navigable. You could tweet things, and people would respond and retweet them. You could put up witty Facebook statuses, and all your friends would comment on your wall. (Remember typing updates start with ". . . watching TV right now" because Facebook put "Jason is . . ." in all your updates? That was silly.) And YouTube, well, I didn't start uploading my own YouTube videos until 2009, but I watched endless videos and commented on them, and the video creators responded. (What a novel idea! Actually talking with someone on *social* media!). The social media party wasn't yet in out-of-control proportions, and you had time to stay for one or two more drinks.

Near the end of 2010, the floodgates opened up. Marketers and brands created accounts like they were going out of style. Groupon was dominating people's inboxes (I bought more tooth whitening $40-for-$20 deals than I care to admit). Pinterest was just getting popular with its invite-only registration tactic (a brilliant marketing move that still works to generate buzz if your product is actually great). I even made the switch from my personal profile on Facebook to a brand page because I had hit the cap of 5,000 friends on my account (one of the dumbest things Facebook ever did in my opinion; capping at 5,000 friends). In short, the social media house party seemed to be bursting at the seams, and it was getting harder and harder to move through the party, let alone hear anything anyone was saying.

In mid-2011, the party erupted like the Icelandic volcano Eyjafjallajökull (which coincidentally, had just erupted a year prior in 2010). Instead of spilling molten lava and spraying volcanic ash for hundreds of miles, the social media party erupted with brands, marketers, and social media experts flying in every direction. They had deals, offers, sales, follow-for-follows, e-books, and so much more. And there I was, caught in the middle of it. My little social media marketing company IWearYourShirt was no longer the new kid in town. Less people were actually talking to one another, and it seemed like everyone was just trying to sell something.

Don't get me wrong; IWYS shared offers, deals, and sales, but we did that as sparingly as possible. We tried to focus on building relationships with brands and with fans, telling stories and creating unique and engaging content for people to enjoy. My issue is that the majority of people using social media forget all about the *social* part of it. Twitter isn't the classified section in the back of a newspaper or magazine. Facebook isn't a new fancy billboard. These sites were built for interacting and creating two-way conversations, not for getting people to save 15% on their next pair of stupid skinny jeans. (Truthfully, I'm only mad at skinny jeans because my legs are too husky to fit in them.)

IF YOU BUILD IT, THEY WON'T NECESSARILY COME

I've seen it time and time again: people think if they sign up for a Twitter or Facebook account, fans and customers will come running. This is delusional. When I originally started IWYS, I spent tons of time emailing my contacts—contacts that I had built relationships and trust with for years. And even those folks didn't drop everything and line up to give me money and praise. It's certainly not going to happen overnight in the crowded landscape of today's social media.

If your products or services aren't selling before you get on social media, the likelihood of your Twitter account helping you sell those products or services is about .0001% (for those of you who aren't *Math-Magicians*, that's very, very low). Social media channels like Twitter, Facebook, YouTube, Instagram, etc., are all separate networks for a reason and should be treated as such. One of the biggest mistakes people make is signing up for every network. I do believe you should own your brand name on each network, but that doesn't mean you have to be actively using each network. Another mistake is linking your social media accounts together (posting the exact same content on Facebook, Twitter, Instagram, etc.).

Think back to the idea of a party. If you attended three separate parties, and said the exact same thing and wore the exact same outfit, you'd get laughed at (or ignored). It's the same way with social media, except the social media wrongdoers are ignoring the telltale signs (limited or zero interaction on certain platforms). Attend each separate party (social media channel) with unique content or messaging. No one is forcing you to use every network. And spreading yourself too thin without a strategy for each can have a negative effect. When you try to use 12 different networks without experience and a well-planned strategy for each, they all fail. It might not happen immediately, but after a few months, there will be little to no engagement. I'm not trying to be Debbie Downer here; I'm just stating the facts. As mentioned earlier in this book, your business strategy, your website, and your email marketing plan should all come first. When you have those things down to a science, *then* start thinking about using social media, and start one network at a time.

MY SOCIAL MEDIA SCREW UPS

When I was first drafting this chapter, I laid out a plan to talk about each social network individually. I was going to share my thoughts on how to set up goals for each network, how to use them, how not to, and give an example of someone doing it right. Then my awesome book writing coach, Lizzie, said "Hey Jason, that's super boring, don't write that!" Okay, so she didn't actually say that at all (she's pretty much supportive of any idea I have). But it got me thinking. There are many books out there on how to use social media. There are many case studies available that you can learn from: what works and what doesn't. And honestly, that all sounded pretty damn boring and not like something I wanted to write about in *my* book. So instead, I'm just going to share a couple stories with you of mistakes I made using different social networks.

MISTAKE #1: MY NAME IS JASON, AND I BOUGHT FANS ON FACEBOOK

Believe it or not, I didn't create a brand page on Facebook for IWear-YourShirt until late 2009. Granted, Facebook Fan Pages had just come out a few months prior, but because I essentially *was* IWear-YourShirt, I didn't see any value in having a separate page. But one day, on Ustream live video, a bunch of IWYS fans talked me into it. (I was always a pushover for the IWYS fans.) With some hesitation, I created the IWearYourShirt Facebook Fan Page and made it live.

I was excited because I thought it could be a new avenue for me to promote the companies on my shirts and to interact with our fans. For the next few months, I shared random photos of me in t-shirts on the page that I didn't share on my Facebook profile. Each day, I shared a link to where I was on live video. And that was about it (riveting, huh?). During those months, there was some fan growth, but it was slower than the steady growth I saw with my Twitter followers, YouTube video views, IWYS website views, and of course, Ustream live video.

I got discouraged about the Fan Page. For a few more months, I watched the page grow to about 1,000 fans. Some of you may

Señor Sangria has a special limited surprise for you. Take a photo of this page and post it with #SenorSangria.

be saying *"Jason, 1,000 fans, that's awesome!"* You are 100% correct, person reading this book, and I firmly believe that even having 100 fans is great. However, on this day, I was "people hungry" and needed more fans to feel good about myself. NEED MORE FANS!

I had heard through the social media grapevine that brands were buying fans in droves. I reached out to a few friends and asked if anyone knew about "growing a Facebook Page by spending a little money." I felt kind of like someone buying illegal drugs by asking the question in that vague way. (Let it be known, I don't buy illegal drugs and illegal drugs do not equal buying Facebook fans. Also, don't do drugs.)

One of my friends got back to me and knew of a guy who knew of a guy (isn't that always the way?). Through the course of an email introduction, I met my drug, err, *fan* dealer. I responded to the email introduction by saying I wanted to know how much Facebook fans cost, and if the accounts came from the United States or around the world. The response from "my guy" was that he was serving fans from all over the world, and that some accounts were real, and some accounts were fake. RED FLAG, JASON! Fake accounts? That was a thing?

I was taken aback by the realization that people bought nonexistent fans for their pages, but my desire to have a higher number of fans on my Facebook Page was at an all-time high. MORRRRRRRE!

My assumption was that IWYS was cool, and through whatever method this guy was sending fans my way, more *real* ones would come than fake (so naïve, so naïve). Then the pricing came. For $500, I could get 750 fans. For $1,000, I could get 2,000 fans. And for $2,000, I could get 5,000 fans.

IWYS was doing pretty well at the time, and I knew I wanted our Fan Page to seem impressive. I bit the bullet and agreed to the

$2,000 option. (Listen, I know what you're thinking. Looking back, it was a stupid waste of money, but that's why I'm sharing it with you in this section of my book! Learn from my mistake!)

To say I was excited was an understatement. *My guy* said the fans would be delivered over the course of the next month to make sure nothing looked fishy. Just the fact that he had a plan to make things not look fishy should have been another red flag. During that next month, I watched the Fan Page grow. Each day, I'd check the page to see the total fan number get bigger and bigger. My cravings for more fans were being quenched, like Dracula's lust for human blood. The other thing I did that you can't do on Facebook Pages anymore was look through the accounts of people who were becoming fans. Here's another giant red flag for you guys. I must have clicked through over 1,000 of the Facebook accounts that became fans, and not a single one looked like a real person. They had a blurry photo, a name, and lived in obscure countries around the world.

During the rest of the month, I watched the IWYS Fan Page grow from 1,000 fans to well over 7,500 fans. The extra gap in numbers was organic growth (which I should have been happy with) and some "extra" fans *my guy* threw in with the deal. Note: I posted the same exact quality and volume of content, because I obviously wasn't going to change what I was doing to get fans now that I had purchased a ton.

Before my purchase, I had 1,000 fans and 100 people liking a status or commenting on something. After my purchase, I had 7,500 fans with 200 people liking a status or commenting on something. With an additional 6,500 fans, I had only doubled my interaction? There was no way. Something didn't add up and that something was the fact that ALL of the fans I bought were fake accounts. I clicked through a countless amount and never found a profile of a real person. I felt like a complete douche-a-saurus-rex (a wonderful term my buddy David Siteman Garland made up). Here I thought I was going to pull one over on the world and have this impressive Facebook Fan Page for IWYS. Instead, I had just flushed $2,000 down the toilet. Worthless. Virtual. Facebook Crap.

A couple fans noticed the spike and asked about it. I played it off by attributing it to some big press hits (which I was getting, I promise those were all real!). Deep down inside my soul, I was crushed.

Back in the day, people were so concerned with Facebook numbers (and a lot still are) and I fell prey to that. Not only did it muddy up the page because there were thousands of inactive fans, Facebook eventually starting finding fake Facebook accounts across tons of pages and deleting them. Over the years, I'm guessing the majority of those fans have been removed. Luckily for IWYS, there was enough organic growth from real human being fans (THANK YOU) that the total number basically leveled off, and I didn't have to admit this to the world. So what's the moral here? Don't cheat the system. Even today, people are buying fans for their pages, and some are even doing it through Facebook ad campaigns. I don't know of any Facebook pages that have grown a real audience of people, who interact daily, through Facebook ads. If you don't purchase fans and are getting new fans on your page, you KNOW they are real people. Every single one of them. You should do your best to provide those real fans with great and unique content, and hope they interact. Don't worry about the stupid vanity metrics. Don't let your ego get to you.

Before telling you this story in this book, maybe three people knew this. Honestly, it feels good to share such a terrible (and expensive) mistake. But it taught me the value of true fans. Really

Good Life Granola is an Artisan Blend manufacturer of delicious granola using the best ingredients. One taste and you will say: I <3 GLG!

passionate fans can't be bought . . . they are earned (like most other great things in life). From that point forward, I made it a point to focus less on the number and more on the quality of the relationships I was building.

MISTAKE #2: @ REPLYING EVERYONE WITH THE SAME MESSAGE ON TWITTER

In 2011, when the IWYS sales weren't flowing in as steadily as in years prior, I hiked up my trousers (who calls them that?) and decided to put my nose to the grindstone again on Twitter. At the time, IWYS was seven people, and I was trying to juggle managing them while also handling my daily t-shirt wearing duties. Those were full-time jobs themselves, so taking on additional outreach efforts was going to be hard to fit in my schedule.

A brilliant idea popped in my head, and I thought, "people don't look at all your @ replies on Twitter, so I'll just send a ton of the same messages to different brands and no one will be the wiser!" Ugh, just typing that made me feel super icky. Anyway, I crafted a message that I thought would entice companies to buy days on IWYS and had to keep it short (with Twitter's 140-character limit and all). I ended up with something like "@companyname ever heard of IWearYourShirt? Would love to wear your shirt, make videos, and have fun! http://iwearyourshirt.com" (Again, ugh.)

So I had my message and then took to Google to find a list of brands on Twitter (easy to find). Once I found the list, I started firing away! One small smart thing I did (by accident) while committing this massive Twitter spam mistake was that I sent these tweets late at night (like after midnight late). That wasn't actually the time I had planned, but it was the only time I had. So I sent the tweets out, and got about 100 of them before I got a message from Twitter that scared the crap out of me. I don't remember it exactly, but it went something like *"You're tweeting a bit too much, we're putting you in time out for 60 minutes."* Whoa. Talk about feeling like the Twitter police had just caught me and put me in temporary Twitter jail. My heart dropped into my stomach and I knew I had to slow down (not stop, obviously—just slow down).

After the 60-minute timeout, I got back on the tweet train and sent another 100 or so tweets over the course of several hours. By about 4:00 a.m., I sent over 250 brands the same copy-and-pasted tweets. I was exhausted and went to bed, thinking I'd waking up to a bunch of purchases or responses.

A few hours later, I woke up and scrambled to grab my iPhone off my nightstand. The glowing light lit up my face as I opened my email to (I hoped) a bunch of days purchased. There were none (I bet you weren't too surprised). Saddened, I thought maybe because I sent the tweets so late that people hadn't read them yet. I opened the Twitter app and noticed I had some new @ replies of my own.

Now's where it gets juicy . . .

You ready?

. . .

. . .

. . .

. . . .

(This is the only way to build a dramatic pause in a book.)

I had @ replies, but they weren't the ones I wanted. Maybe two brands had written me back saying IWYS wasn't the right fit for them. Then there were 10–15 brands that replied back but asked why I had spammed them and tons of other brands with the same tweets. $#&T! I was caught red-handed. Not only had some of these brands not appreciated the unsolicited sales-spam, they had looked at my @ replies and noticed I had sales-spammed a bunch of other brands as well (with identical messaging, need I remind you). These responses couldn't have been further from what I had hoped for. Here I thought I was embarking on some secretive sales efforts only to find that not only did it not work, it made people angry!

As quickly as you can say *Jason that was stupid*, I went in and deleted all of the 250-ish identical @ replies. With each individual click on the delete button, I felt more and more awful about what I had done. Yeah, okay, it's not the worst offense in the history of social media, but it was the complete opposite of what I had hoped would happen. It felt like jumping into a hot tub on a cold night, expecting the water to be hot and comforting, but instead finding the tub full of ice cubes that are filled with liquid nitrogen. Yeah. That would suck right? With all the tweets deleted, I still received a few more @ replies (because the tweets still appeared in some people's open Twitter feeds), scorning me for my sales-spam. Each one made me feel worse.

I learned a valuable lesson about Twitter and about spamming people. First, people can spot a spammy sales tweet from a mile away. As Gary Vaynerchuk says, "people's bullshit radar has gotten really good." Second, I learned yet another lesson: you can't short-cut your way to success, even if you're using a social media platform that sends short messages. Unfortunately, I'm not the only person who has committed this type of Twitter crime. Sadly enough, some of you reading this may have committed this offense at some time or another. I implore you to never do this again if you have done it, and never to think about doing it after reading this story. Use Twitter to engage with people. Use it to start conversations. Use it to build meaningful relationships. Heck, use it just for customer service. That is the intent of Twitter, and that's what works really well. The sales will come. If there's a silver lining to this mistake, it's that you can learn a lot by just doing things. Yeah, some of those things might not be so great, but trial and error is one of the best teachers in life.

MISTAKE #3: THAT TIME I SIGNED UP FOR KLOUT AND CHECKED MY "KLOUT SCORE"

Yep. That's the mistake. Moving on.

MISTAKE #4: CHANGING FROM REAL CONTENT TO COMMERCIAL CONTENT ON YOUTUBE

It may not necessarily be a social media mistake, but I think it fits to share here. Whenever I get asked the question, "is there anything you'd change about what you did with IWYS over the years?" I often say I wouldn't change anything, but when backed in a corner, I talk about this "mistake."

Sometime in 2010, through a combination of questions from IWYS sponsors and my impatience to make a viral video on You-Tube, the daily videos I created changed from what I was doing in my life to branded commercials. In essence, I went from a guy living his life and sharing his daily escapades through YouTube videos, to a guy making two- or three-minute long YouTube advertisements. I want to be clear that I am damn proud of the videos I made over the years. However, I think my YouTube *career* would have been very different had I not changed and gone the branded commercial route.

What I think was so successful and interesting about IWear-YourShirt in the early days was the voyeuristic snapshot it took of my life. I wasn't doing anything amazing on a daily basis, but I had a unique personality and wasn't afraid to goof off on camera (or in public). This entertained people, and because I wasn't a celebrity, there was a certain relatable feeling people got when watching me. I went to Target like anyone else would, but I just happened to lay down in the aisle with a video camera and try out new pillows for my bed. When I started making branded commercials, I was fortunate to have built up a sizable audience that didn't abandon ship when the video content gradually changed. They stuck with the shift in content of the videos, and I was still being entertaining (call it goofy or funny). But over time, the YouTube videos had almost nothing to do with my life and were solely focused on the message of a brand. While I loved telling the stories of the majority of brands I wore t-shirts for, the video content lost some of that *realness*. It lost some of that unique quality people could relate to.

I don't have any hard data to compare what the difference would have been had I done less commercial-style videos on You-Tube, but I'm certain things would have been different. Video bloggers were popping up left and right on YouTube as the platform became more and more popular (and accessible due to video camera technology and affordability). Many of these video bloggers who shot up in fame and notoriety weren't doing anything different from what I was doing in the beginning of IWYS. Yes, some of them had beautiful, swooping bangs. Yes, some of them ate 30,000-calorie meals in one sitting (Epic Meal Time is crazy!). And yes, some of them were attractive girls talking about their lives. But as I watched more and more of these personalities come out of nowhere on YouTube, and I wondered "what if?"

Stafford & Son, Spiller Me Timbers, Show Me Your TDs, Sidd Finch All-Stars, Here's my number..Call me Brady, Mike Ehrman-Trout, Luck Dynasty

You can "what if?" yourself to death when it comes to social media and different aspects of starting or owning a business. The fact of the matter is, I'll never know what would have happened had I continued to do more real video content on YouTube. And that's okay. As I mentioned, I'm still very proud of the videos I made, even if they were more commercialized than I would have liked. Maybe sticking with real videos would have been a disaster for me? There's no way to know, and I'm certainly not going to dwell on it. From this experience, I've learned to stick with my gut—be happy with whatever decision I make and make sure it answers the question, "what if?"

So WHAT'S NEXT WITH SOCIAL MEDIA?

If there's one thing I'm 100% certain about, it's that "social media" will be around for quite awhile. By the time you read this book, Facebook might have become the next MySpace, and SnapChat may have replaced text messaging on our iPhone 77s. Either way, you should get on board in some capacity. You don't need to use every social network that pops its head out of the sand, but you should, at the very least, investigate them (and maybe grab your brand's username, just in case). You might find that using Facebook brings you incredible value and is crucial to the success of your business because you have access to a larger network of people to try to reach. You might find that Twitter lets you create unique connections with your customers that you'd never be able to manage via email (which can be incredibly beneficial for service-based businesses). Maybe Google+ is the social network for you. Do you make physical products, or is your business based on a creative process that's primarily visual? I'd highly recommend trying out Instagram.

That's right. Jason knows how important mobile technology is for business. You should too. Work with Myriad Mobile and work with the best.

The point is that you should find the right platform that matches up best with your product or service and give it a try!

No one has the perfect formula. There are resources out there that will help shorten your learning curve, especially if you're new to social media, but the majority of your education will come from trial and error: doing things, seeing how those things work, and iterating going forward.

Social media is crowded these days. *Billions* of people crowded. Remember that when you're getting started, but also remember there are huge opportunities right at your fingertips.

Keep up the creative thinking and day dreaming! Feel free to tweet me! Best, @TheNiceBrian

Chapter 19

LET'S DO
~~LUNCH~~ LAUNCH

SPONSORED BY GOTOMEETING

One thing I put a ton of effort into with every new business I create is my launch strategy. With years of experience under my belt, I can safely say that an effective launch strategy can make a gigantic impact on your business. Some people prefer to simply put up a website and "soft launch" their projects, waiting to see who comes trickling in. I get it; it can be scary to put it out there to the world and say "Hey! I'm launching this thing on this day! Come check it out!" But the truth is, by building buzz and deeming one recognizable point in time important, you're increasing the likelihood that people show up. There's a greater feeling of excitement and you can use that to your advantage.

A great launch strategy works both for your website and a new product or service. I've had several successful project launches, not because I'm lucky, but because I've had a strategy in place for all them. There's a process I've identified when it comes to building

Online meetings are better because you can stay home when bad weather or illness strikes and still attend your meetings.

buzz and preparing people to buy things, and I use it for every single idea I have.

There was a time, however, that I didn't have a launch strategy in place . . .

A few years ago, I started a non-profit company with a focus on donating t-shirts. Not only did I learn a lot about the non-profit world and the dos and don'ts of the mission of a non-profit (this is for another book or a conversation over copious margaritas), but I also learned the importance of setting a launch date. With IWear-YourShirt, I had a concrete launch date for the project, but it more so fell in my lap because I knew I wanted to use the 2009 calendar as my sales platform. With the non-profit I started, I didn't have that. So what happened? Well, I came up with initial plans for the company and started to put things in motion (becoming a 501c3, having a website built, creating a marketing plan, etc.). What I *didn't* do was set a specific launch date or actionable goals (daily, weekly, monthly). Every time I started working on something to do with the non-profit, something else distracted me. I put off working on the non-profit planning because it didn't feel as important as my other tasks.

Three months of procrastination went by and barely anything was done, which included that I still didn't have a simple informational website built. In contrast, you may remember that the IWearYourShirt website went up only a few weeks after the initial idea (and that included a full e-commerce and content publishing platform). It didn't have anything to do with my motivation for the non-profit project either, because it was a huge idea and I was incredibly passionate about it.

I'm sure you've experienced this in areas of your life. When you don't have a set time or date to get something accomplished, it always drags on. I eventually got the website finished, wrote a marketing plan, and launched the non-profit, but it took six months.

It bothered the heck out of me that it dragged on for so long and when the project finally launched, I realized how much time I had wasted—time I could have spent marketing and making a difference with this non-profit. Was it the end of the world that the process dragged on for six months? No. But it did feel like I was carrying around a 600-pound silverback gorilla towards the end of the launch. Every task and to-do item felt cumbersome. Taking forever to launch *that* project has made me diligent about setting launch dates for any other project I approach, and I make sure I do everything I can to hit those dates.

Let's look at an example of my process when it comes to launching something, but instead of IWYS (since we've already discussed it and we want to *avoid* those mistakes), we're going to pretend your talent is making great popsicles, but that your niche talent is making delicious, beer-infused popsicles (obviously known as BeerSicles).

We're going to further pretend that the BeerSicles website is launching in three months. Remember what I learned from not having a launch date? Set a date on your Google calendar, your refrigerator—heck, tattoo it on your body somewhere. Wait. Don't do that tattoo thing. That's a horrible idea. Anyway, let's get started with your planning!

STEP #1: EVERY CREATIVE IDEA NEEDS A GOAL

This may sound mundane and obvious, but there are a lot of people who start things without an end goal in mind. They think, *"Hey, I'll launch this project, and XYZ will fall in my lap or happen by chance."*

Start hosting your own face-to-face online meetings today. Get a free 30-day trial of GoToMeeting by visiting GoToMeeting.com

Good luck with that. I went that route for one day in October 2008 with IWearYourShirt and it sucked. You need to take charge. Come up with goals, write them down, and keep yourself and your company accountable to them.

When I initially thought of IWearYourShirt, I didn't just think of it as something I would do in 2009. I had big goals to grow to 10 people in 2010, then to 50 people in 2011, and even hundreds in 2012. Did those goals pan out? Nope. But without having initial goals like that, I may have just worn shirts in 2009 and stopped there. You need big goals to inspire you and keep you pushing forward. Your goals will change. You won't meet your goals. But the goal with goals is just to have them and strive for them (I tried to fit the word "goal" in this sentence again, but couldn't figure out how to do it).

How many BeerSicles do you want to sell in week one? Month one? Year one? How are you going to do it? What are your plans to convert sales through your website, through social media, and through other outlets? Can BeerSicles be sold in local stores? Want to be in Whole Foods? Want John Mayer to eat a BeerSicle while singing "Daughters" in Las Vegas? Okay, maybe not that last one. We'll answer some of those questions with Steps 2–8 (not the John Mayer one, unfortunately).

STEP #2: EMAIL MARKETING IS YOUR BEST FRIEND (YOUR BFF!)

Have I beaten it into your skull how important your contact list is? Well, that list of personal contacts can either stay separate from your email marketing plan or be included. Either way, you should immediately sign up for an email marketing client when launching your company. I recommend MailChimp and have used them

Online meetings are better because you can meet immediately as needs come up, since you don't have to travel to meet.

religiously for my different projects over the years. It might be the cute monkey mascot, the amazing customer service, or the fact that it's 100% free up to 2,000 email subscribers (it's a great problem to have when you need to pay for more!).

I want to share a little story of how one of my email marketing lists (of only 623 people) netted me over $10,000 in ONE hour.

When I was planning to sell my last name for the first time in 2012, I knew the project was going to shock people when it launched, but I didn't want to give away the project itself before the launch date. What I ended up doing was creating a simple landing page that was an email capture. Here's what that teaser website looked like for BuyMyLastName:

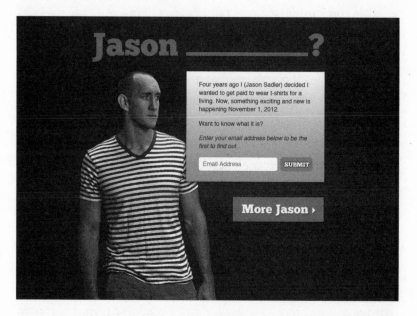

Super simple, right? As you can see, I was very clear about what someone would be getting if they signed up for my pre-launch email list and when the launch would be. The steps I took behind the scenes to create that email marketing campaign are fairly straightforward with MailChimp:

> I already had a free account, so I made a new List.
> I used their insanely simple Form Builder to create a sign-up form.
> I used the same Form Builder to customize my Opt-In message (when someone submitted their email), my Thank You message (when some clicked the confirmation link in their email), and the First Email message (the first email from me by subscribing to that list).
> I grabbed the Embed Code in MailChimp and easily plugged it into the website you see above (the one with my photo and sign up box)
> BOOM! I was ready to rock!

That was it! I was off and running, ready to promote this teaser page and email sign-up for BuyMyLastName. I promoted this page through my different social media accounts and even other mailing lists. What I promised people who signed up for this list was EXCLUSIVE access to this new project when it launched, giving them time to view it before the general public.

I launched this teaser website and email sign-up two months before BuyMyLastName.com launched and the bidding war for my last name would start. In those two months, the subscribers of that list went from 0 to 623. I'm not going to lie; I was a bit disappointed that I didn't get more subscribers. We all want bigger numbers right! (Quality, not quantity, Jason!)

Well, when I sent the email to this list on November 1, 2012, an hour before public launch of BuyMyLastName.com (as I had promised), I was surprised. The open rate of the email was incredibly high (around 80%, when industry standard is around 10–20%), and these people knew they were getting an exclusive look at my next project and took advantage of that. Within an hour, a handful of email subscribers from this list had bid my last name auction up to $10,000 before the rest of the world even saw the website!

I watched the bidding price climb and people from that list replied to my email with praise. I felt excitement, relief, and proud of my efforts. When I did tell the rest of the world, people were completely shocked that the price was already that high on an auction that started at $0 an hour prior.

I know that pre-launch email list was crucial for BuyMyLastName. I also know that a pre-launch email marketing campaign for BeerSicles (or whatever your awesome business idea is) will be immensely beneficial as well. Whether it's MailChimp or some other email marketing provider, this should be a huge focus for your launch plans.

Note: *You might want to set calendar reminders of when you want to send emails to your list so you stay consistent. You should also set a reminder on the day of launch that tells you to share with your email list first. I didn't have anyone managing my email marketing, so it was important to have additional reminders.*

STEP #3: WHAT'S YOUR PRE-LAUNCH MARKETING PLAN OUTSIDE OF EMAIL?

There are so many social media websites, forums, blogs, local events, etc., out there. It's important to create a list of them and pick which

Online meetings are better because you can attend meetings all over the country and world all in one day.

ones you think will bring you the most value. Let's say you're going to use Twitter to promote BeerSicles at launch and going forward to update customers about new flavors and things happening with your company. Here is a list of questions you should answer:

> Do you have a dedicated Twitter account for that company, or do you want to use your existing account? (For a consumer product, I'd recommend its own account.)
> Who is going to run the account?
> How often do you plan on updating it?
> What type of content can you tease people with in the months leading up to your official launch (photos, videos, interviews, etc.)?
> Can you find any Twitter chats for new startups, for beer related companies, or for local conversation in your area?
> How can you provide value and a unique experience for your followers (not just telling them your products are for sale)?
> Is there a pre-launch group people can join to get exclusive access and perks?
> Do you like when I ask lots of questions with bullet points?

Ideally, you'll answer the same questions for other launch outlets (social media sites and things offline, too). Start a Google Doc, Word Doc, Evernote, or even write the answers to these questions down in a physical notebook. The key here is to *get started way before launch*, and work on building a following or creating some buzz.

BeerSicles would benefit from Instagram (#craftbeer and other beer related hash tags are very popular). Find a local photographer and pay them to shoot photos for an entire day. That one day could give you beautiful BeerSicle Instagram photo content for months

@PRisus on easily connecting to international customers: "Gotta love @Go-ToMeeting for these international client conference calls across time zones!"

to come. Imagine all the magnificent filters you could apply to your Triple Espresso Milk Stout BeerSicle!

And hey, maybe you don't want to use social media at all? That's perfectly fine, too. Will your local Chamber of Commerce help you? How about local Rotary groups? Any local creative or entrepreneurial groups that will help you get exposure? Are there small business groups in your area that hold meetings? If you're opening a physical retail location, you'd better put some creative "Coming Soon" signage up for people walking by. No matter what avenue of promotion you choose to use, be methodical about it, and start generating buzz early on.

I know this may seem like a big task, but the rewards you'll reap by being prepared and starting early will be great. The launch date for IWYS was January 1, 2009, but I started promoting and planning in October 2008. Those two and a half months were CRITICAL for me launching with nearly 180 days sold on my calendar and over 1,000 Twitter followers. Oh, and I didn't have a strategic plan like I'm laying out for you in this chapter. I didn't even have a book. I scrambled around like a chicken with its head cut off, just doing stuff and hoping things would work. It was a complete mess, but I used the techniques described here and they worked. Now I live by this type of planning!

STEP #4: CREATE ADDITIONAL CONTENT TO BUILD BUZZ

When I first started writing this book, I talked to a fellow entrepreneur named Natalie Sisson. Natalie had used Kickstarter to crowdfund her book (in a completely different way than SponsorMyBook). One thing she did while running that Kickstarter project and eventually publishing and selling her book *Suitcase*

Online meetings are better because people may be more likely to join since they don't have to host someone in their office or drive to a different office.

Entrepreneur was to create a Pinterest board. That Pinterest board served as a place for her to showcase fan-submitted photos holding and reading her book around the world. When anyone submitted a photo holding her book, she'd upload it to her Pinterest board. When she first told me about this, it gave me the idea to do my Visual Author Journey on Pinterest.

The idea behind the Visual Author Journey Pinterest board was to have a dedicated place where I shared behind the scenes thoughts, feelings, and updates while I wrote the book. I took photos holding up Post-it Notes describing my feelings on that day's writing. I shared music I was listening to while writing. If my dog Plaxico was helping me write (read: sitting on my lap begging for attention), I quickly snapped a photo and shared it.

I created this board not just to drum up extra buzz, but also to share content that was exclusive to Pinterest. There were multiple times I shared a photo from Pinterest to my Twitter account, but that was in attempt to make sure people knew I was putting unique content there. I also shared my Pinterest board with my email lists. I wanted to make sure people knew the Pinterest board existed and that I was keeping updates unique on every site.

The goal of the Pinterest board wasn't to help me sell thousands of copies of my book; instead, I wanted to have a visual diary of the process of writing a book. Maybe you've seen that Pinterest board, or heck, you bought a copy of my book because of it? Either way, it was one notch in the pre-launch marketing plan for this book.

Just like I mentioned earlier, I think Instagram would be a fantastic option to create buzz for BeerSicles. Maybe you picked a certain beer you love, so share a photo of it. Maybe you're trying out different popsicle sticks, so share a photo of you holding them so people can't see what they are and they have to guess. Use appropriate

@theadamoliver on tending to customers from anywhere: "Working from anywhere in Savannah! #GoToMeeting allows me to easily assist customers this week."

hash tags and other accounts to gain attention from people outside your immediate following. Get my drift here? Use content to keep people interested and engaged, and include updates telling people to sign up for your email list or follow your new @BeerSicles Twitter account for customer service or additional content.

STEP #5: FIND THE INFLUENCERS!

Hey reader, do you remember that story I told you about Grasshopper.com and how the company sent those 5,000 gross chocolate covered grasshoppers to influencers? That's what we're talking about here! But let's break it down and look at the nuts and bolts that go into making something like that happen.

The first thing to do is to find influencers (bloggers, social media people, news outlets, magazines, websites, etc.) who write about your industry or product. I like to use a Google Spreadsheet to keep track of lists like this (you could use a similar spreadsheet for doing pre-sales, launch parties, etc.):

	A	B	C	D	E
1	Person	Email Address	Company	Website	Contact Date
2	John Doe	john@aol.com	The Beer Guy	JohnLikesBeers.com	1/2/2014
3	Mike Smith	mike@gmail.com	Mike's Beer	Mikeandbeer.com	1/2/2014
4					
5					

F	G	H	I
Respond Date	Shared? Yes/No	Notes	Link?
1/8/2014	YES!	John loved IPA BeerSicles	http://johnlikesbeer.com/beersicles-rock
1/4/2014		Thinking about it...	

With a spreadsheet like that, customize it based on who you are reaching out to and what's important for you to monitor. The example might just be for beer blogs on which BeerSicles could

Collaborate with anyone, anywhere. Start a free 30-day trial of GoToMeeting by visiting GoToMeeting.com

potentially be featured. You could create another section for people or companies you hope to have tweet about BeerSicles.

When you're building this list, it's important to remember one key thing: DON'T OVERSELL! The soft sell goes a long way. Think of this like going on a date for the first time. You aren't just going to try to hit a metaphorical homerun when you first meet. No, you're going to take your time and lay on the smooth moves (maybe with some Barry White playing in the background).

Since you love beer, you probably follow some people on Twitter who also love beer. Before you ever try to pitch them or ask them to talk about BeerSicles, spend a few days or weeks engaging with them on Twitter. It may feel a bit stalkerish, but hey, even stalkers need to sell beer-flavored popsicles. Once you feel you've built a rapport on Twitter, reach out to them and ask them if you can email them some inside info on a new cool product you're launching. If you've done a good job, and played the right Barry White song, they'll most likely join without hesitation. You might even find that they stalk your Twitter profile and find the website link you put in your Twitter bio that goes to your pre-launch website with an email capture (and then they sign up!).

When you do email these influencers, don't pitch them; just share the idea, and ask for feedback. Ask if they're interested in trying your product before anyone else. Especially do this with people who have passionate followings.

Next, look for people who write about beer and get lots of comments on their blog or stories or through interactions on Facebook or Twitter. Have others written about beer on Mashable or other tech blogs? They'd love to know that you're using the Internet to sell an innovative new product! The key with any type of influencer is to build relationships that can help you on launch day.

Online meetings are better because taking notes on your computer during an online meeting beats taking them on a notepad that you'll eventually lose anyway.

STEP #6: LOCAL PRESS CAN BE HUGE

Most people ignore local press because they want the big dogs like *The Today Show, Good Morning America, CBS Evening News,* etc. What you don't realize is there's an entire media network behind the scenes that's owned by a lot of the same companies.

In February 2011, I received a very exciting email. It was from a producer at *The Today Show.* HELL, YES! Talk about one of the best emails that can come through your inbox. Not only was I overjoyed by the opportunity, but also I figured this was going to be my next big break for IWearYourShirt. I enthusiastically responded YES to the question from their email that asked, "Could we come to your house and do a story about your unique t-shirt business?"

A few weeks later, the producer, Durrell, who I still keep in touch with, a cameraman, and an on-air personality by the name of Sarah Haines showed up on my doorstep. You know how ridiculously overjoyed kids get for toys at Christmas? That was how I felt when I opened the door and let them in. For a few hours, we talked about t-shirts, we hung out in my closet, we hung out in my office, and it was over in a blur. The excitement didn't wear off after they left. For the next few days, I was on cloud nine. But then a funny thing happened. My segment didn't air in February. Then it didn't air in March. After three months, I was beginning to lose hope. Luckily, the producer was awesome about it and let know my story was definitely going to run, but they just had to find the right timeslot for it (this happens often with "feel good" stories).

And then it happened. I got the email on April 28, 2012, that my segment was finally going to air the next day. Back to cloud nine I went! Maybe even cloud 10 or 11! That evening, I got zero sleep. I lay in bed with the covers pulled up tightly to my chin. All night I thought of all the people who would email in about how awesome the IWearYourShirt piece was. I thought about how I'd sell $10,000 worth of IWearYourShirt days (being conservative, of course). In the morning when I woke up, I watched every minute of the two hours that led up to my segment on *The Today Show* (mine was the very last—hey, last but not least, right?). Then Sarah Haines (the reporter who came to my house) said, "I have to tell you about this guy who gets paid to wear t-shirts for a living in Florida . . ."

Intensely monitoring Facebook, Twitter, and website traffic on my laptop, I watched the segment they filmed about IWearYourShirt and me. A few text messages poured in. There were a handful of tweets and a bunch of congratulatory messages and comments on Facebook. The website traffic steadily increased from a couple hundred to over a thousand people. Then 2,000. Then 3,000. Then a day sold on the calendar. Then another. And then . . . it was over.

As soon as the segment had come on screen and ended, so had the traffic, the sales, and the buzz. My dreams of making $10,000 amounted to about $800 in sales. My hopes of an explosion of emails in my inbox was less than 100 people who all poorly wrote in saying, "I wanna get paid to wear tees." Just like that, it was over. I had built up insane expectations, only to be left with an empty pit in my stomach (somewhat like the original *NYTimes* article about IWYS). And while I did try to leverage *The Today Show* story after it was over, it simply didn't have the same effect because I had already received so much press the previous years.

At the same time, I was waiting (patiently, I might add) for *The Today Show* segment to air, a local news channel filmed a segment on me. In late March of 2011, the very talented news anchor Lewis Turner came to my house and filmed a segment for *First Coast News* in Jacksonville, Florida. Lewis is a great guy and probably one of the best media people I've ever worked with . . . and I've worked with a lot. He's also a one-man-band (like most local news anchors) and is the producer, cameraman, and on-air personality. I'll admittedly tell you that I was way less excited about the local news segment (who wouldn't be with a *Today Show* interview looming?). After trading a few emails with Lewis, we met at a location a few miles from my house at the beach. We filmed a segment about IWearYourShirt, which was very similar to *The Today Show* story, and that segment was going to air the same evening.

I won't lie to you: I tried to be enthusiastic and excited while being interviewed by Lewis, but in the back of my mind, I assumed the local segment was a blip on the radar compared to the massive *Today Show* interview.

As the rest of the day went on, I had almost forgotten about my local interview. I flipped on the TV and watched the segment. (I will say that no matter the size of the media outlet, it's pretty freakin' cool to see yourself on TV.) The story Lewis put together was really great; it hit all the important points about buying days on IWYS and the fact that I was hiring new Shirt Wearers in a few months for 2012. Lewis nailed it. Then I checked my email and actually had three calendar days purchased. I was shocked but excited. The website traffic increase was minimal, but I received a handful of encouraging emails from local Jacksonvillians who appreciated the idea, signed up for my email list, and loved what I was doing. I felt really good about this local exposure, but knew *The Today Show* was going to be the money-maker (you already know how that turned out).

But then the funniest thing happened. About a week later, I got an email from someone in Denver saying they had seen me on their local news. What? I hadn't done a local news segment in Denver.

Online meetings are better because you don't have to book a conference room.

I was confused. Then someone from Portland emailed. Then Cincinnati. Then Dallas. Then another, and another, and another. Over the course of that week, I received emails from people in 27 different cities. The website traffic for the week was over 60,000 visitors, and in total, 10 days had been purchased on the IWYS calendar. I emailed Lewis and asked him if he knew what had happened and he said, "Oh yeah, there's a whole syndication network behind the scenes with local news, and if a story does well, other cities will pick it up and run it." And oh, how they did!

I was shocked by the exposure that one local news segment could bring and had no clue it had the potential to do so much more than *The Today Show*. The local news segment had brought in 10 times the money and 20 times the website traffic. Hard to believe, right? Well, believe it. And while I'm incredibly grateful for both, I'll never doubt the power of a local news segment again.

But Jason, what actionable things can I take away from this experience for Step #6 in this chapter? Thank you for getting me back on track, creative person reading this book!

Maybe you don't know local press folks in your area, but you *can* watch the news and see if they're on Twitter or visit their website and see if they have places to submit news or ideas. Local news stations want to talk about cool stories in their area. Use that to your advantage and give them some advance notice, but not so much that they forget about you. I recommend trying to reach out to local media 1–2 weeks before launch to see if they'll do a story on you or your business (remember to pitch the local angle, even if it's an Internet business!). I wish I had some secret information to share with you about getting on *The Today Show*, but alas, I think that was just luck created by all my hard work over the years. You don't need luck or years of work to get featured by local media.

They're itching to talk about your BeerSicles! (Or, whatever the real business is you're starting or currently running.)

STEP #7: ONE WEEK OUT, TAKE MARKETING ACTION!

Start some serious marketing ONE week prior to launch. Give people an exact time to look forward to. I personally like 10–11:00 a.m. ET, but you can choose something that works well for you. Make sure you share that launch time with all your networks, email list(s), etc. At this time, you should have a landing page or something simple up on your website that tells people the time of launch. Don't forget your email list gets first dibs, so make sure they know you're launching at 11:00 a.m. ET to the public, but they'll know at 10:30 a.m. ET because they've been loyal subscribers.

Remember what happened with BuyMyLastName? The prelaunch list was instrumental for my launch, but I also emailed them a week before to remind them the launch date and time was coming. I also reminded my Twitter following and Facebook audience, and I sent out hundreds of carrier pigeons to all the castles in my realm.

STEP #8: LAUNCH THAT SUCKER! I MEAN . . . THOSE BEERSICLES!

Make your website live, send out your launch email to your list(s), contact the influencers on your list, Tweet it, Facebook it, Instagram it, make sure local news knows today is the day, and yell out your window really loudly, although preferably not all at the same time. Undoubtedly, something will break or not work; be honest about it with your audience and update your list accordingly.

During the launch of one of my endeavors over the years, I had a brutal mishap. I had done everything you've read in Steps 1–7, and the time was upon me to share with the world this awesome thing! I was amped up. I was on the edge of my yoga ball (I sit on a yoga ball—not a chair—you should try it). I was doing everything I listed at the beginning of Step #8 to announce the project to the world. I was brimming with excitement, waiting for the money and accolades to come pouring in. But instead, I got a ton of frustrated emails from people.

"Jason, I can't give you money!" and

"Jason, the thing you are trying to sell isn't working for me!" and

"Something is wrong with your website, you jerk." (That last one is 100% real).

Crap! I went from excited and happy to sour, fast.

Somewhere along the way, I had forgotten to check the status of my e-commerce platform to make sure it was out of TEST mode and ready for actual purchases. Dammit! Unfortunately, I thought my developer was going to handle this. Double Dammit!

Either way, I launched the website to thousands of people, and none of them could buy. For two hours, people couldn't give me money for the thing I had created buzz about for months. I was mortified. I remember my girlfriend sitting in the office with me (along with my dog Plaxico) and as reassuring as she was, I felt like I was sitting alone on a deserted island. Yeah, okay, that's a bit dramatic, but when you pour your heart and soul into something, it gets emotional when things don't go as planned.

Those two hours were awful. It may not seem like a lot of time in the grand scheme of things, but two hours is a gigantic time window when you're doing a build-up launch like we're talking about in this chapter and especially with the short lifespan messages have on social media these days. [Side note, if you were doing a soft launch,

Online meetings are better because video conferencing makes it feel like you're meeting in person, since you still see facial expressions and gestures.

where you just put something out into the world and slowly shared it, this might not be an issue.] Eventually, it was figured out that the TEST mode setting was the culprit for all the issues that people were emailing about. When we figured that out, the purchases finally started coming in, but I was upset. For two hours, I had missed out on people spending their money. That was an opportunity I was never going to get back. Maybe the majority of them ended up being patient and buying, but I'll never know how much money I missed out on.

I don't share this story with you to scare you, but to make sure you check and double check everything. Get someone else to look at your project and test it out for you. I learned a valuable lesson with that project launch failure, and I make sure to test thoroughly nowadays. Also, be ready all day launch day to answer questions, fix orders that get placed wrong, walk someone through a simple process that a four-year-old could do, etc. Even though I had a big mishap with the launch of that project, I was able to salvage many of the customers because I was keeping everyone updated on social media and email.

Once your project is launched and running smoothly, keep the ball rolling. Keep updating people, keep sharing content, keep working hard, and don't give up if you don't make $1,000,000 in your first week. Work towards those goals you set for yourself and your business, and make new ones along the way.

If you notice, launching your website or your next product involves a lot of the same thinking as getting started on social media. You simply can't expect to put something out into the ether and hope people find it. There's just too much stuff and competition in the world right now for you not to have a strategy in place when you launch.

Want to increase your sales close rates? @Sharefile did by 34% with Go-ToMeeting - just by turning their webcams on!

Thank you to my friends at GoToMeeting, who have graciously sponsored this entire chapter. I've worked with GoToMeeting since the early days of IWearYourShirt, and their online meeting platform is something I rely on heavily when it comes to organizing product launches and keeping things running smoothly. Be sure to check out GoToMeeting.com, and sign up for a 30-day free trial!

Chapter 20

TEKST CASE STUDY

We've gone over a lot of information in these last two sections, but I don't want you to just walk away from this book with a list of bullet points; I want you to feel confident about making it work for your business. That's why I also want to share with you the story of how I helped a friend of mine take his niche talent—creating awesomely unique pieces of art made from words—and turn it into a highly profitable living. Hopefully, through this chapter, you'll be able to see all the pieces we just talked about come together in a practical, real-world way.

TWO GUYS, ONE AIRPORT OUTLET

One March, I sat in the Austin, Texas, airport, the sunshine streaming in through the huge windows. As I waited for my flight, I reminisced about the good times I'd just had at the SXSW Interactive Festival. I was hung over from partying too late the previous night, but I should remind you that SXSW is the *biggest geek party in the world*, so the "partying" is relative. Nonetheless, my head was pounding.

At my gate, I found a perfectly isolated row of chairs next to a walkway. It also had an electrical outlet, which is a hot commodity

Carter Law Firm | Help for Geeks & Entrpreneurs | Contracts, Copyrights, Trademarks, Social Media Law, & Flash Mob Law | CarterLawAZ.com

in any airport terminal. I plugged in all my Apple devices so they could get charged up, and I put on my headphones to attempt to shut out the world.

Minutes later, out of the corner of my eye, I notice a guy walking my way. He was a normal enough looking human being, wearing a t-shirt and jeans, a wardrobe choice of which I clearly approve. He wore a hipstery trucker hat and flip-flops, so I assumed he was most likely a fellow SXSW attendee. When I realized he was coming straight for me, and upon further visual investigation, saw that he was carrying a very recognizable white MacBook power cord in his hand, I cringed.

Maybe he didn't notice I was already using both of the outlets, or maybe he just assumed I wasn't an only child. Either way, I pulled back my headphones as he got closer and held up his Apple cord.

"Any way I can use one of the outlets to charge my laptop?"

There were two responses that came to mind. The first was a simple: "Sure, man . . ." and I could be the nice guy. The second option that crossed my mind involved me pretending to speak a lost (read: unknown) Nordic or Viking language, which would (hopefully) force him to give up his pursuit.

My conscience won out, so I shrugged my shoulders and scooted over.

"Sure, man." I unplugged my phone charger, and he plugged in his.

Some of you might assume this is the part where I put my headphones back in and go back into my own world. Well, think again.

Unfortunately, the designers of cords at Apple had doomed me on this day. Apple didn't make power cords in "let me plug this in and sit a few rows away" length. No.

They made this cord mighty short (4–6 feet!), which meant I

now sat directly across from random trucker-hat guy.

I'm not opposed to talking to people, but after a week of schmoozing at the biggest event in the interactive industry, I was ready for some quiet time. He was now sitting two seats away from me in the row of chairs I had spread my bags across in hopes of deterring other people. (For the record, I'm a typically very friendly human being . . . but a headache and dehydration and geek hang-over can really drain a guy.)

Because we were sitting so close to each other, the small talk was inevitable.

"You go to South-By?" he asked while unpacking his laptop and plugging it in.

"Yep, you?" I replied, huddling a little closer to my things to give off some body language that I was tired and wanted to be alone with my electrical outlets.

"Yeah, it was crazy. I'm Jason by the way." He said, leaning in for a handshake.

(Well, look at that! This guy might not be so bad after all!)

I sat up a bit. "I'm Jason as well, how about that? Enjoy South-By? First time?"

"Oh, nice! Yeah man, it was a blast. I'm a bit hung over, the par-ties were way more than I expected at a tech conference," he joked as he adjusted his hat and sat back in his chair.

(Alright. He's earning more cred here, earning more cred.)

"I hear ya. After Iron Cactus and Buffalo Billiards, I'm feeling pretty rough." I laughed while remembering my one-too-many mar-garitas and vodka drinks. (Damn you margaritas and vodka drinks!)

"Oh yeah, I checked out the Mashable party there . . . it was nuts. Good times. Where you flying to?" he asked.

"Actually . . . San Diego." I sighed and let my cheeks puffer-fish out to emphasize my exhaustion. "Heading to another conference, but this one will be quite a bit less crazy than South-By. You?"

He sat forward. "Wait, really? Do you live in San Diego? I'm flying there, too, and that's home for me."

(At this point, I've warmed up to my fellow Jason. I mean, we were both named Jason, and we were both feeling the pains of drinking with crazy geeks. What's not to like?)

"Nope, don't live there. Just speaking at this conference and hanging out for a few days. I actually grew up outside San Diego in a little town called Rancho Peñasquitos." I diverted my full attention from all my Apple devices to my fellow Jason.

"Nice, man, I know right where that is. I'm in Carlsbad. What's the conference, and what are you speaking about?" he asked.

"It's the San Diego Advertising Digital Marketing-Something-Or-Other, and I'm just talking about my business and social media," I said, trying to skirt around the issue of talking about IWearYour-Shirt. Back then, I tended to skirt around the issue of sharing IWYS with complete strangers; I wanted to avoid feeling braggadocious—or wonder if they thought I had lost my mind and made the whole thing up.)

Of course, other Jason asked. "What's your business about?"

I took a deep breath. "Well, I actually started this company called IWearYourShirt.com, where I get paid to wear t-shirts for companies and promote them through social media. It's kind of weird."

He responded very simply, with confusion and disbelief. "Nuh uh!"

I reassured him, "No, really. I've been doing it since January 1, 2009, and have worn over 500 branded t-shirts so far and gotten paid for it."

"No &^$#ing way! REALLY?" he airport-whispered-yelled.

I grabbed my laptop off the chair between us, quickly typed in

IWearYourShirt.com, and spun the laptop around to him. "I swear!"

Other Jason's was, at once, dubious, excited, shocked, and again, confused. In my experience of telling people about IWYS for the first time, this was a fairly standard reaction, and I had dealt with it on many occasions.

Right around this time, Southwest began boarding our flight. If you know anything about flying Southwest, you'll know there isn't assigned seating. We were still mid-conversation and on the same flight, so we sat next to each other and continued chatting. While I enjoyed our conversation, I also used him to occupy a middle seat next to me so I wouldn't end up next to some smelly ogre. Hey! We've all been there! Plus, I'm 6'5" and about 235 pounds. You won't find me shopping in the Men's Petite section at Banana Republic.

During the flight, Jason told me he was consulting but wasn't in love with his work. He had a few clients and was able to pay his bills, but he wasn't happy, and he certainly wasn't living the life he wanted to live—and I empathized, since it hadn't been that long ago that I had felt the same way. I wanted to find a way to help Other Jason, but we were both busy. When we landed in San Diego, he and I exchanged phone numbers and went our separate ways, and our friendship turned into one of digital acquaintances . . . and that was that (or so I thought).

SOUTH BY MARKOW

In March of 2011, I attended SXSW again (are you noticing a theme here?). At the time, I hadn't talked to Jason Markow (see "Two Guys, One Airport Outlet" for a refresher) in a few months, and I didn't know if he was going or not. On my first evening walking the downtown streets of Austin, who do I see standing in front of a Mongolian beef restaurant (that I was planning to eat at) with a few people? Jason *freakin'* Markow.

For reference, in 2011, SXSW had nearly 50,000 attendees. The college I attended in north Florida had only 10,000 people, and I barely ever saw friends I knew when I was on my college campus. Needless to say, it was quite a surprise to see Jason on the first night, and I joined his group for dinner.

The group was a mix of cool people I'd never met. A really nice guy named Mouyyad Abdulhadi (who sponsored page 163), a nice girl named Laura Kimball, who worked for HTC a few years later. And then, there was a really young-looking kid with shaggy hair. He wore his SXSW hoodie and backpack but did not fit in. (General rule of thumb, folks: wear the free swag conferences give you *after* you leave the conference.) I later found out this shaggy young fellow had randomly joined Jason and his friends earlier in the day and hadn't left their sides. He didn't know them, and I think at one point his Dad was there, too. Odd, I know.

Dinner was great—good conversations and lots of delicious Mongolian beef (I love me some stir-fried Mongolian beef!). The the next day at the Pepsi Foursquare outdoor lounge, Jason and I met up as we'd agreed to at dinner the evening before. He had a business idea he wanted to share with me.

We sat at long plastic benches under the Texas sun and watched people play real-life competitive games of foursquare (If Sam Taggart and AJ Vaynerchuk read this book, note that I remember you taking foursquare very seriously!). Geeks and hipsters alike were sprawled everywhere. There were beanbag chairs, more benches, tents, and thousands of people walking the streets of downtown Austin.

Jason began to tell me how inspired he was by me after our

meeting in the airport in 2010—my making a living wearing t-shirts, using social media and a unique pricing model. Recently, he'd been messing around with a style of art that used words to create shapes and negative space. He opened his notebook and his laptop, and shared some unique sketches of his work. His foundation was to take words and reshape the letters to help create a bigger image.

To Jason's credit, he had actually already made 40 pieces of art in this new style and was going to try to sell them in local galleries. He had been talking with a few mentors and friends and was trying to create a unique business plan around this style of art he called: TEKST Art (TEKST like "Text"). As I listened to his passion for this new project (which was the opposite of how he talked about his consulting business the year prior), I thought it would be a great fit for the $1 per day incremental pricing structure I had come up with and used for IWearYourShirt. I grabbed a nearby napkin and started scribbling.

In a matter of minutes, I had drawn some numbers on it, a wire-frame for a website that would sell his art, and explained how I thought this was one of the few ways I'd ever thought the incremental pricing structure I had created with IWearYourShirt could be re-used. With TEKST, it could feel truly different from what I was doing. By this time, he (and most of the people who had heard of IWearYourShirt) knew that the $1 per day pricing would net him $66,795 at the end of the year.

Note: *Many people had tried to copy IWearYourShirt by this point. There were at least 50 copycat websites I had seen, and I'm sure there were a ton more. Not only that, but people had tried to start IWearYourHat, IWearYourPants, and other iterations that all failed.*

Note #2: *I never planned to branch out to IWearYourHat, IWearYourPants, etc. Instead, in 2010 and 2011, I had locked in yearly "Proud Partners" that paid me to wear their brand's clothing with my t-shirts. Thank you Jockey Underwear, Blacksocks.com, and Lucky Brand Jeans. Seriously.*

As I slid Jason the napkin and finished my spiel, the look on Jason's face was a mix of surprise and joy. Here he had come to me with an idea to try to sell some art, and in a few minutes, I'd shown him how he could create a new way to sell art online and potentially make some good money. I did explain that it wouldn't be easy, though.

"You can do this, and I believe it'll work, hands down. But it's a big undertaking. Not only are you going to have to create 365 unique pieces of art, you'll also need to hustle to sell them, ship them, make sure your customers are happy, and build an audience so you could do this for longer than one year."

Even though I laid down the honesty, his face beamed. "Also, 365 pieces of art is just be the tip of the iceberg. Just watch. You can create the art, and it doesn't require promotional hours like IWear-YourShirt. Selling art this way is unique and can help you get commissioned artwork that you can then sell for a much higher price tag."

Jason looked at the napkins for a moment and looked back up at me, speechless. I continued. "You can potentially get some big sponsors on board that would pay to be associated with your project and get exposure to an audience primed at buying art, you know, like art supplies."

He laughed. "Here I wanted to sell 40 pieces of art, and you show me him a way to sell 365 pieces of art, plus two other potential streams of revenue." Without much more to say and a whole lot of resolve, Jason was pumped.

Starting from scratch. Help me decide what to build and follow the process of starting a business from scratch. gerlandopiro.com/creative

We stayed in touch the rest of the SXSW trip, meeting up a few more times and chatting. He asked questions about how to build the website, and even joined me for one of my Ustream live video shows from a hallway in the Austin Convention Center. The more we talked about this new business for him, the more excited I was to try to help him make it a reality, and the more excitement he generated to get out of his lackluster career in consulting. It made me wonder if there were other people out there like Jason who just needed some inspiration and some outside perspective to nudge them in the right direction. (If you haven't noticed yet, that's the entire point of this book.)

Over the next few months, we had weekly phone calls, exchanged countless emails, and talked about sponsors he should approach. I helped him build an email marketing plan for the launch of the project. (If you haven't done so, check out LaunchRock.com for a great email capture website. It's a **completely free** service that let's you set up a simple landing page with name and email submission forms. Remember back when I said your contact list was your most important asset? This is one way to grow that list before your project starts.) We talked about different ways he could film the creation of his art and upload those videos to YouTube to use as daily content for his website. I think I even made a few suggestions for art pieces that ended up getting made and sold! I will admit those were far and few between. I remember emailing him motivational quotes and making suggestions like, *"you should totally draw this awesome quote into, like, the ocean with a mermaid or something!"* Obviously, I was much better at the business strategy advice.

By November of 2011, Jason Markow had built a pre-launch email list of nearly 500 people. He had done so through emailing his contacts and directing them to his LaunchRock page, as well as by reaching out to his existing social media accounts (Twitter and Facebook). Jason had also secured a sponsorship with an art supply company that provided $14,000 worth of canvases and materials (hell, yeah!). He had built a small following on Twitter and Facebook, and had even put up a few teaser videos on YouTube that gave a glimpse of the style of art he would be selling. He launched the TEKSTartist.com website and offered a pre-sale of his TEKST art calendar of 365 pieces that would start shipping on January 1, 2012.

ON THE DAY OF LAUNCH, JASON MADE $11,000. IT WAS THE MOST MONEY HE HAD EVER MADE IN ONE DAY.

On the day of launch, Jason made $11,000. It was the most money he had ever made in one day. Heck, he made more money that day than he typically would over the course of a few months. By the time January 1, 2012, came to an end, he had already sold hundreds of pieces of art (some of which were commissioned pieces). By the end of the year, Jason was only working on his art and was making triple the income he was making as a consultant the year previous.

Jason made over $100,000 selling art in 2013. He moved away from the $1 per day pricing model in 2014 and adopted a $5 incremental pricing model for a site called FiveSpotDerby.com. Like I did from 2009 to 2010 with IWearYourShirt, Jason added another new twist to his pricing model and the way he sold art online.

Jason didn't have much of an audience to start. Jason had an idea, the drive to see it through, and the ability to weather the storm of entrepreneurial ups and downs that were bound to happen. One of the things I wish I had that Jason Markow has is the ability to create something out of thin air. If you have the talent to create something and want to make money doing what you love, you can easily become the next Jason Markow.

This letterpress design features a two toned ink and foil image created from the text that makes up the following quote by Chuck Palahniuk:

"If death meant just leaving the stage long enough to change costumes and come back as a .new character . . . Would you slow down? Or speed up?"

TEKST Astronaut by Jason Markow – www.5spotderby.com

Use mega-hit movies to teach leadership. Each DVD with 50 clips and lesson plans. LeadershipInTheMovies.com For teachers, coaches and ...

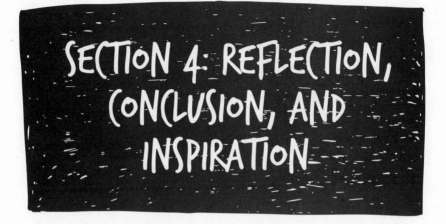

SECTION 4: REFLECTION, CONCLUSION, AND INSPIRATION

We're nearing the finish line, folks. This is the last section of the book, and I want to share some of the "deeper" stuff with you. The wild ride I've been on with IWearYourShirt and my other ventures has led me to some conclusions about what I think is important in life, and I've made some big life changes as a result.

CeliacandtheBeast.com is the gluten-free place to be for learning about living life with celiac disease and non-celiac gluten sensitivity.

Chapter 21

MISFITS

In the spring of 2013, I was in a bit of a funk. IWearYourShirt hadn't grown into the massive global t-shirt wearing empire I had imagined, and I had announced I was retiring from wearing t-shirts. That point in my life felt very much like those days back in high school cafeterias, standing in the doorway with no place to sit. I felt quite lost in my life and didn't really know what I was going to do.

Right around then, my good friends AJ and Melissa Leon (find them on page 186) organized a small event to bring people from all walks of life—misfits—together in an attempt to "make a dent in the universe," and they called it the Misfit Conference, or Misfit Con, for short. Melissa asked me to speak at the event and talk about my success with all my unconventional businesses. There was a bit of irony that Melissa had asked me to come share my story, since I wasn't feeling too successful at the time. Because I valued Melissa and AJ's friendship so much, I agreed to speak and figured I could bury my feelings and get through the event with a smile on my face. Little did I know what was to come.

When I arrived at Misfit Con in downtown Fargo, North Dakota, one of the first people I saw across the quaint art gallery (that was hosting the event) was a familiar face: Pamela (Pam) Slim.

Few things are more critical with your creative project than great branding and an awesome website. We'd love to help @ DesignExtensions.com

The last time I saw Pam was back in March 2011, while I wandered the streets of downtown Austin, Texas, at SXSW. I spotted her through the crowd back in Austin, and when I did, I diverted my path directly toward her. She saw me coming, mostly because at 6'5" tall, I'm hard to miss. We'd never met in person before that day (only chatted via social media), but Pam swung her arms open wide and gave me a hug like we were long lost friends. Since that first meeting, I've always felt a warm sense of friendship from Pam, and I was glad to see that she had also decided to attend Misfit Con.

Once again, I made my way toward Pam and she swung open her arms and gave me a big hug. This encounter, however, was different. Pam and I were both attending Misfit Con as speakers, but no one attending the event was labeled as anything other than a "misfit."

Pam took the stage early in the event, and it was the first time I heard her tell her story. She talked about experiencing cultures around the world, being in difficult relationships, figuring out what her values were, what her talents (ingredients, as she calls them) were, and what brought her happiness and the feeling of success in life. She shared a touching story of a school renovation that her father had worked on and the lessons she learned from it. I'm not an emotional guy, but Pam's personal story and the story of this school renovation touched me. I found myself wanting to know how Pam had figured all this stuff out. How she had overcome her adversities, and how she had looked within herself to figure out her values and unleash her talents onto the world?

To remind you, at that time, I was in a tough place mentally, emotionally, and financially. I didn't know it at the time, but hearing Pam's talk completely changed the talk *I* would give at that event. I had initially planned on talking about all my successes (like I normally would), but instead, I wanted to tell people where I really was in life. None of my talk was planned, scripted, or premeditated. I wanted the audience to know that from the outside, I looked like this super successful entrepreneur, doing what I loved and having loads of money in my bank account, but on the inside, I was the exact opposite on all fronts. I was in debt. I wasn't happy at all. I had gained back a bunch of weight that I had painstakingly lost less than a year prior. I wasn't going to lie to this small group of people. I was going to tell them exactly how I was feeling and what I was going through. I sat down for a Q&A session with Srinivas (Srini) Rao, a surfer who had made a name for himself conducting interviews for his site BlogcastFM (now: Unmistakeable Creative), but I don't remember much else besides a leather stool on which I sat and the small black stage, with Srini sitting across from me on another stool, his coffee in one hand and a microphone in the other.

READING THIS BOOK AND FEELING LOST? DON'T HESITATE TO SHOOT ME AN EMAIL: JASON@SPONSORMYBOOK.COM

An audience of about 50 people, including my girlfriend, Caroline, stared at me, ready to hear all about my success and how happy I was. It was the first time I'd ever felt close to vomiting before talking in front of an audience (and I'm never that nervous or have that type of feeling before talking in front of people).

Srini asked me to tell everyone a little bit about my backstory. I answered with an abridged version and let people know that this talk was going to be different from what I normally did. About 45 minutes went by that I don't remember much of, other than trying to hold back tears while pouring my heart and soul out to these complete strangers. That, and a question from Srini about what I had been like as a kid, with my response being a joke about getting an "unsatisfactory" mark when it came to "speaking out in class."

Before I knew it, the talk was over. Srini thanked everyone, and when I looked out at my fellow misfits, almost everyone was standing up and clapping. It was an odd moment, as it felt like I snapped back into reality and had no memory of the previous hour except for small fragments. I could see Caroline off stage clapping, and I realized that prior to that hour, she was really the only person who knew what was actually going on in my life and in my head.

You know when people talk about getting "a monkey off their back?" I felt like I had shed an 800-pound lowland silverback gorilla from my back. Oh, and did I mention that gorilla was carrying another gorilla on his back? Yeah, it was a ton of weight that seemed to just evaporate from my body. There I was on stage, in a room full of strangers, and I had just been more vulnerable with them than almost anyone before in my life.

I have to give AJ and Melissa credit for creating an event that allowed me to feel safe enough to pour my heart out. That moment was the first time in a long time that I felt I was in a place where I could share my real thoughts and feelings without judgment.

Why tell you all of this? Because immediately after I got off stage, Pam came up, gave me a big hug, and said she would be there for me if I ever wanted to talk (a big part of Pam's business is life coaching, and not the sleazy kind). It was reassuring to know I had people around me that were willing to help me figure things out. Though I still felt just as lost as I did before, I finally felt like maybe that was okay. Maybe part of being an entrepreneur is acknowledging when it doesn't all work out the way you had planned. Opening up like that was the first step in what would be a new chapter for me.

DOES THIS THING BRING ME VALUE?

There were many other talks at Misfit Con that made a huge impact on me. One of them was by a tall slender gentleman with majestic hair named Joshua Fields Millburn. I didn't know Josh or his story; I only knew that he dressed well and looked like a young Christopher Walken (seriously, go Google his name and find a photo of him). As Josh began to tell his story, I felt an emotional tidal wave come over me. Josh talked about how he had one day realized he worked at a job he hated, that he was in a huge amount of debt, and that he wasn't happy and was continuing to try to fill the emotional void in his life with *stuff*. And then he started to make changes. He got rid of almost all his worldly possessions. He created a strict plan to pay down all his debt (which wasn't fun for an entire year of his life). He stopped worrying about what society had told him success should look like, and he started looking within himself.

One thing Josh said is something I ask myself almost every single day: "Does this thing bring me value?" That question applies to friends, to material possessions, to the work you do, to nearly every aspect of our lives. Josh finished talking and I wanted to rush up and give him a hug (a totally acceptable bro-hug, obviously), but I didn't. I was too afraid to tell him that I was living the life he had escaped. Instead, I wrote down some notes in my notepad and started to think about my life and the decisions I was making.

Misfit Conference was a truly life-changing event for me. I made many new friends and built stronger bonds with existing ones. On the flight back home to Jacksonville from Fargo, Caroline and I talked a lot about our lives, the work we were currently doing, the people we were surrounding ourselves with, what we really wanted to be doing, and what brought us happiness.

Caroline said this was the most emotionally open she'd ever seen me. And it was. I was tired . . . Frankly, I was freakin' *exhausted* from carrying around all this emotional baggage and bottling up all these feelings and negative situations. It was time to let some of them go.

My previous blog, JasonSadler.com, had been my personal hub online for years. Up until that point, I had shared ramblings about social media and marketing, updates about my life, and other random things. For the first time, though, I decided to share some *real* feelings with the world. I wasn't going to pretend everything was perfect anymore. It started with this blog post I wrote on June 3, 2013, after we got back from the conference, and it's a post that I think captures my frame of mind after that experience:

AFTER AN AMAZING WEEKEND AT MISFIT CON, I FEEL LOST . . .

It's safe to say that Misfit Con was the best conference I've ever been to (and I've been to quite a few). Not only were my fellow speakers amazing and inspiring people, but so were the attendees, and the folks behind the conference. AJ and Melissa Leon put together an outstanding event, in Fargo, ND and their attention to detail was mind blowing. I don't want to recap the conference; I want to explain why I feel lost after such an amazing weekend.

You see, I'm at a bit of a crossroads in my life right now. I run a business that's currently in a state of ambiguity, but it's also a business that was previously very successful. IWearYourShirt has been my life-blood for the past 4½ years, it's changed me as a person, it's brought about awesome opportunities, helped me meet tons of great friends, let me build a fantastic community, but after this past weekend, I'm lost.

Let's back up for a minute. In 2007, I left the 9-5 world to start my first entrepreneurial venture. I took a big risk leaving my secure job that I didn't really enjoy to do something else, something I thought I was truly passionate about (co-owning a web design company). As it turned out, I wasn't really passionate about web design, websites, finding great clients, or any of that, I just liked doing it a lot more for my own company than someone else's. Then, I conjured up the idea of IWearYourShirt and took another risk. Except this risk had a much more profound affect on my life. Since 2008, I've been doing something I really enjoy, but am I actually passionate about it? After listening to my new friend Joshua Fields Millburn challenge me to ask new people I meet "What are you passionate about?" (instead of "What do you do?"), I realized I couldn't answer that question myself. This isn't the first time I've had this feeling. In fact, just a few months ago I was talking with my girlfriend Caroline and confessed that I didn't know what I was passionate about. I do know that I'm excited by a bunch of things: food, shoes, IWearYourShirt, cars, design, building stuff, traveling, helping companies, my family, cool t-shirts, the city of Jacksonville, etc. But, I'm not sure I'm actually PASSIONATE about any one of those things in particular. And the majority of

FLBlogCon.com is the "go to" source for all your blogging and social media questions. We'll see you at our next conference!

my fellow Misfit Con speakers have found their passion and are extremely happy. (jerks! Jk . . .)

So what the heck do I do from here? Well, I've had plans in place for the next phase of IWearYourShirt, and I'm going forward with those because I strongly believe in those plans and I love the company/brand I've built. But the direction I'm going in with IWearYourShirt might take a detour here or there. I want to really think about creating value for both Shirt Wearer and Sponsors, and as my other new friend Greg Hartle told me at Misfit Con, I want to feel like I'm actually contributing something to the world. Maybe that happens with IWearYourShirt, maybe IWearYourShirt is simply a conduit to get me there.

I do know this: I want to write more, I want to ask for help from my peers (I'm looking at you, Pam Slim), and I want to share more personal videos that bring you guys along with me on this journey. In the past I would have thought about structuring this in some way, and thinking about optimizing it, but I think that's part of what's been holding me back from finding my passion. I just want to share my thoughts, hear your thoughts, and hopefully find my way. I'm guessing there are many of you reading this who might feel the same way, and maybe even some of my fellow Misfit Con attendees.

Let's not do this alone, let's find our passions together.

It scared the hell out of me to press the *publish* button on that post, and I wavered back and forth between publishing and deleting it for several hours. I finally said, "screw it" and published it anyway. I shared the post on my main Facebook page, but then also in a closed Facebook Group of Misfit Conf attendees. I don't know what response I expected, but the response I got was amazing.

Many of the other Misfit Conf attendees felt the same way but were scared to share. Many of my friends on Facebook had no clue things weren't going well (and how would they). The outpouring of support through comments on that blog post and in emails, Facebook messages, and text messages made me feel so uplifted and validated. I didn't expect or hope for any of that; I had merely wanted to get some of the feelings I was burying deep down out.

From that day forward, I tried to force myself to write a blog post a week that opened up and peeled back another layer. I wrote about "Societal Pressure," where I completely reexamined my life goals and what I thought success meant. I wrote a post titled "Are Our Friends Really Our Friends" which was received differently by some people than others, but I wanted to start removing people from my life who weren't bringing me value. I wrote many of these types of posts and I found that with each one, I felt a little bit better. It was the beginning—I completely changed the way I thought about and lived my life up to now.

After months of sharing through my blog, I finally worked up the courage to email Pam again and ask her for help. Pam and I had exchanged emails right after Misfit Con, but by the time I got back into my routine at home, my emotional walls went right back up, and I was afraid to talk to her. I didn't want her to see me in a state of weakness or think that I wasn't doing well. I put off taking her up on her offer until eight months later in January 2014. It wasn't until I started tearing those walls down brick by brick on the blog that I felt in a much better place emotionally to chat with her (read: I would have sobbed like a baby had I called anytime earlier). I had figured out some of my core values and realigned a lot of my life priorities. It also helped that Pam's new book *Body of Work* (which I highly recommend) had just come out and she'd sent me an advance copy to read. I had read about 15 pages of her book when I sent her an email and asked to chat. She responded quickly, and we set up a Skype call the next week.

Remember that "Christmas Eve" feeling I talked about earlier with IWearYourShirt? This was the opposite. For one reason or another, I wanted the day we scheduled the call to get pushed back as far as possible. Alas, it didn't, and Pam and I jumped on Skype.

During our hour and a half call, I asked Pam a bunch of questions about how to find your ingredients . . . how to really know what your values were. I asked if I was supposed to feel as lost as I did, and if that was normal. Pam's smiling face and nodding head reassured me that I was not alone. She said she'd been there before, and that it's all a part of the journey.

"Jason, where you *are* alone is that this is *your* journey, *your* battle to find yourself and understand who you truly are. Unfortunately, it isn't going to happen over night. Like a business, it will take time, iteration, and effort—and it won't be easy."

I understood what she meant and tried to digest it as quickly as possible. But then she nailed me with something I now tell any entrepreneur who asks me for advice: "You just have to stick with it. You have to show up and you have to not be afraid to make mistakes and learn from them. You also have to realize that your values might change over time and that just when you think you have everything figured out, it might all change. But no matter what, everything is going to be okay."

Powerful stuff, especially during the dark times.

Even as I write this book, and as you read it, I'm learning more about myself. I'm constantly thinking about what things actually make me happy. I'm removing negativity from my life as often as possible. And I'm always asking myself "Does this thing bring me value?"

The world needs more effort, hustle, and execution. Jason, thanks for providing that example to everyone that experiences your work.

Chapter 22

REALIGNING VALUES

When I graduated high school, I had three goals in life:

1. Own a Ferrari by the time I was 30
2. Be worth $1,000,000 by the time I was 30
3. Retire at age 35

Looking back, all of those are pretty silly goals. First, I'm 6'5" tall. I can barely *fit* in any Ferrari, let alone be able to enjoy driving it with 45 mph speed limits everywhere in Jacksonville.

Second, in high school, I had no clue what that $1,000,000 figure represented. Was it net worth? Revenue of my company? Seven figures in the bank? Regardless, I never took the time to think about why I *needed* that much money; I just wanted it.

Third, I picked "retirement" at an early age because I assumed I'd work some crappy job and want to get out quickly. I'm happy to work until I'm 100 years old if I truly enjoy what I'm doing. Let me remind you, those goals were made right when I graduated high school.

Through owning my own business and having financial ups and downs, my eyes have been spread WIDE open when it comes to money. There's this idea in our society that success is measured in fancy cars, big houses, expensive clothing, and luxurious vacations. When I finally thought about those things, I realized I didn't care about most of them at all. I love cars, but you can only drive one at a time, and rarely very fast. I'd love a huge house, but for what? I live a fairly minimalist lifestyle and barely have enough things to fill a 1,500-square-foot home (which is great). Would I love to have multiple homes in locations around the world? Sure . . . but I certainly don't need them to be extravagant.

While I *am* motivated by money, it's not to have ridiculous amounts of it; it's to have plenty to feel comfortable. Once you don't have to think about how you'll pay your mortgage payment, you kind of stop dreaming about a bigger house. When I started to think more about what truly made me happy, I stopped focusing on what other people told me I needed to feel successful. It was honestly a revelation.

I have woken up from that *MTV Cribs* inspired dream (while I do love that show), and now I realize what I care about most. Today, that means having certain freedoms:

1. The freedom to work from anywhere, not tied down to a certain city or office.
2. The freedom to know all my bills are paid each month and not have to worry about them.
3. The freedom to choose how I want to run my business.
4. The freedom to understand that I don't **need** things, I just want them, and that these feelings will often pass (normally when I stop watching TV).

From experience, I can tell you that having debt hanging over your head puts a damper on enjoying these freedoms. You feel shackled to it, and once you get rid of those shackles (pay off the debt), it's an amazing feeling . . . one that lasts longer than the satisfaction of buying some shiny, expensive thing (that probably goes on a credit card).

BY THE WAY, BEING A "MISFIT" IS PRETTY DAMN COOL IF YOU ASK ME.

Another option *besides* credit cards is getting a line of credit from your bank. If you don't have credit card debt, you have a business, and you have a business checking account, your bank will often offer you a line of credit. Don't be naïve; this is the same thing as a credit card, it's just disguised as a less sleazy alternative.

Some lines of credit do offer very flexible interest rates and fees. Unlike a credit card, which charges you a certain percentage rate on all your purchases, some lines of credit cap the interest payment you pay a month as long as you use a certain amount of credit. If you are new to this stuff, I highly recommend you talk to a business mentor or someone who helps small businesses with finance in your local area.

Just remember, keep all the business expenses separate from your personal expenses. And make sure to ask your accountant what type of things you currently pay for that can be paid for by the business and written off on your taxes (e.g., your car's gas, lunch meetings, office supplies, etc.). If you work out of your house and you own your house, did you know you could write off the space you use as an office? Don't just do this because I said you can—consult an accountant, as it's different for each person and business!

You are playing "Sponsor-a-Page Tennis"! Purchase games from Wiggity Bang.com and then go to Page 94.

Chapter 23

THE INSIDE SCOOP OF BEING AN ENTREPRENEUR

Looking back over my time as an entrepreneur, there are things I want to share with you about what it has been like to build my own creative businesses from nothing. From the outside, it seems great to be an entrepreneur. You work for yourself. You have all this free time. You have the ability to make boatloads of money that you don't have to share with others. You don't have any financial over-head. And you're the envy all of your friends. Not entirely . . .

BEING AN ENTREPRENEUR IS ONE OF THE MOST STRESSFUL THINGS I'VE EVER DONE.

Yeah, I'm only 32 years old, but the last six years have probably taken 15 years off my life. Before IWearYourShirt, I had never worked for myself. Every job I'd had was collecting a paycheck and working for someone else. While many people think they have

Sociality Squared is a social media agency based in NYC since 2010. Through content and engagement, S2 helps build communities, organically.

stress at their 9–5 jobs, as long as you're getting a steady paycheck, the stress you experience can't compare to owning your own company and figuring out how you'll pay bills each week (especially if you have employee salaries).

During the first year of IWearYourShirt, I was still doing some work with my previous web design company and earning a paycheck. Yeah, I hustled my ass off to make IWearYourShirt successful, but I never felt the financial stress.

It wasn't until 2011 when I had six people's salaries to pay each month (totaling over $20,000) that I really felt entrepreneurial pressure. Each week (almost *each* day) felt like a battle to get enough money for that month. I must have spent 300 of the 365 days in 2011 worrying about money and how I was going to pay all my bills. There were many nights when I stared at my bank account and wondered how I'd make it happen. There were nights when I desperately wanted to go to sleep, but I knew if I just responded to 25 or 50 more emails, IWearYourShirt might make enough money for one person's salary the next month. At one point, IWearYourShirt had $30,000 in money owed from sponsors, and I had to borrow money from my family to pay the monthly salaries (which I had to reduce for one month). I hope to never experience the terrible feeling I had in my stomach when I called each IWearYourShirt employee and told them they'd be getting paid a little bit less that month due to a rough patch with the company.

Sitting in a hotel in Nashville, Tennessee, one by one, I had to call and disappoint the people who trusted that I would pay them what I said I'd pay them when they took the job with IWYS. It really sucked. And of course, hindsight is a beautiful thing. I would have definitely structured the IWearYourShirt payment model differently, or had the salaries follow the income structure of the company, or even let someone go to save a couple thousand dollars each month. At the time, I didn't let anyone go because I didn't want anyone (especially potential sponsors) to think IWYS was struggling. That could have been disastrous for the business.

Like I've said before, I don't regret the decisions I made, and those are lessons I learned the hard way and am glad I learned them. Who knows, maybe I'll own a company with 100 employees one day? And if I do, I'm going to be completely removed from payroll, hiring, firing, and well, anything involving employee management—it's just not my strong suit.

BEING AN ENTREPRENEUR IS ONE OF THE MOST GRATIFYING THINGS I'VE EVER DONE.

There's something magical about owning your own company and seeing it become successful. That success doesn't even mean making money, although that's part of it. But when you create something from nothing and hear people saying positive things about it, or get your first satisfied customer, or make your first month's rent in sales, there's nothing quite like that feeling. Even in the last year of IWearYourShirt, I smiled with every calendar purchase email that came into my inbox. It wasn't just the money. With each purchase, I felt like someone said, *"Jason, I appreciate what you've done with this creative business."* That feeling of appreciation can go a long way (especially when you're selling days on a calendar for $1, $8, $22, etc).

One other incredibly gratifying part of being an entrepreneur is actively being able to see your efforts pay off. When you work a 9–5 job, you can work 80–100 hour workweeks and no one bats an eye (or even pays you overtime if you're salaried). But when you

Hey, I am Cody Strawn from envd.us (a free way to promote your store). Hope you are enjoying this book like we are! Keep on reading!

own your own business and put in extra effort, you almost always see the benefits. You make more money. You get more press attention. You have happier customers. You get tangible feedback for your efforts. I remember way too many late nights working for other companies and never feeling like the extra effort was noticed or appreciated. Even while writing this book, I saw my efforts pay off. When I launched the Supporter spots (at the end of the book— thank you supporters!) the response wasn't what I expected from my email lists and social media. I was actually kind of bummed out. Were my fans not interested in seeing their names in my book? I knew they enjoyed my projects and had supported me before.

Instead of just sitting around and sulking, I grabbed my phone and pulled up Facebook. I spent two hours chatting and texting with people and sharing the link to the Supporter purchase page. In the 24 hours after I launched the Supporter spots, I had probably only sold 25 spots. In the two hours I spent chatting and texting, I sold over 75 spots. It felt amazing to put in extra effort and see it pay off.

BEING AN ENTREPRENEUR HAS CAUSED ME TO LOSE FRIENDSHIPS.

Running and owning my own business has been tough on my previous friendships. I've lost and alienated a bunch of friends, some of whom I'd known for 10+ years. Some of those friends have even become "enemies." Albeit, we don't have medieval sword battles or anything, there are a handful of people I'm not on speaking terms with anymore.

It's tricky to mix friends and business, and I've learned this lesson the hard way a few times (you'd think I'd learn after the first time!). This one particular friend and I had a solid friendship when we started working together. Everything seemed to click, and I felt like I could trust and rely on this person. Then, we had a miscommunication and a bit of an argument. If you've ever worked with a friend or family member, you probably know that these arguments feel 100 times more emotional. I remember feeling like my friend was trying to take advantage of me and accusing me of agreeing to something I hadn't. That miscommunication led to the person ignoring phone calls and emails. With each day that passed, I felt myself getting angrier and angrier about it. Then I'd see the person's name on social media sites (because we were friends), and every status update and tweet brought me closer to turning into a muscle-bound green monster with a building-crushing temper (JASON SMASH!).

A few weeks passed, and we finally got on the phone. What I thought was going to be a constructive conversation ended up in more yelling. Thinking back on it, I bet it looked a lot like what you'd see on reality TV these days. The yelling turned into more anger and—in a matter of minutes—a longtime friendship had ended. It was yet another terrible feeling and experience I hope never to have again.

BEING AN ENTREPRENEUR HAS GIVEN ME THE OPPORTUNITY TO TRAVEL.

A few years ago, I was asked to speak at a conference in Vancouver by Jeff Ciecko (see Jeff's page sponsorship on page 167). Jeff had been a previous IWearYourShirt sponsor and supporter. When I received the email from Jeff, I was thrilled.

Not only do I love doing public speaking events, but also I had never been to the Pacific Northwest. Yeah, it wasn't traveling to some remote island in the middle of the ocean, but I'd heard great things about Vancouver and had always wanted to go.

Because Caroline worked for me at the time, it was the perfect opportunity for her to join me on the trip. When I told her I had landed a speaking gig in Vancouver, she was happy for me. When I asked her to go with me, she was ecstatic! Not only would this be her first time going to Canada, but her first time in the Pacific Northwest as well, and this was the farthest she'd ever traveled in her life (I know, I know, it's not thaaat far from Florida).

Within minutes of telling her, she had already popped open Google and started looking at photos of Vancouver. Smiling ear to ear, she clicked through different photos of the skyline, the harbor, the surrounding mountains, the suspension bridges, and more. I looked over her shoulder just as excited.

The day we left for the airport was similar to any other day. Our business was completely virtual so when we got on our flight, we used in-flight WiFi (what an amazing invention) and continued to get all our work done. When we landed in Vancouver, it didn't feel like we missed any time away from work and were all of a sudden in a completely new city. While we were there, we soaked up as much of the city as we could. We walked everywhere (mostly in the rain, although we didn't care), we ate at delicious restaurants, and we simply enjoyed being in an entirely different city, feeling its energy and drawing it in.

Every time I travel, I enjoy the change of scenery and the new people I meet. If I didn't own my own business (that's run completely online) I'd probably be stuck traveling once, or maybe twice, a year with my standard two weeks' vacation. Then again, my trips are usually always paid for when I travel because I can tie business in (BONUS!).

Being an entrepreneur has been my life for the past few years. And it hasn't been easy. The media makes it out to be glamorous. You hear about all these startup founders in Silicon Valley making hundreds of millions of dollars. But most people don't even make it at all, let alone make millions. I hope by reading some of the stories I've shared in this chapter, it can accelerate your learning curve and help you avoid mistakes I've made. Some of them may seem like common sense, others may be a slap in the face for you (good!). Just know that owning your own business takes dedication and hard work, but it is also extremely rewarding.

And remember, if it was easy, everyone would do it.

Chapter 24

DREAM BIG

No matter where you are in life, you should have big goals. You should have bigger aspirations that you're working toward. From the day the idea for IWYS was conceived, I didn't just think I'd wear t-shirts for a year and be done. I dreamed of five people wearing shirts with me the second year. Then 50 the next year. Then 100 the next. I really wanted to create a new medium for advertising online.

When companies thought about buying banner ads, Facebook ads, display ads, or whatever else, I wanted to be part of that conversation. And I can't count the number of emails and phone calls I received over the years from companies and agencies that weighed the cost of IWYS against other forms of advertising. That was one of the affirming things that helped me see the silver lining through all the mistakes I made.

You aren't always going to achieve your goals, but just setting goals is a huge step toward success. Put in the work, and you'll reap the reward.

lylas.com.au is the fun place to shop! All sorts of applique hand cut & embroidered. Biggest range in the world. Big call just check it out.

Chapter 25

THE HARDER YOU WORK, THE LUCKIER YOU GET

Some version of that "hard work equals more luck" quote has been attributed to Benjamin Franklin, Thomas Jefferson, Confucius, Coleman Cox, Sun Tzu, and many others. The fact is, it's an amazing quote, and if enough of those brilliant people have been known to say to say it, it must be true!

When the first BuyMyLastName auction ended, many people told me I was "lucky" that a company would spend $45,500 on just my last name. Yes, the idea was absolutely crazy, but I had put in a lot of hard work to prove my last name was worth something. What does that work look like?

> › 4 successful years running a company where I got paid to
>   wear t-shirts

> Nearly 40,000 followers on Twitter at an average growth of only 27 followers per day since 2008 (and a Verified account, I still don't know why)
> Nearly 10,000 friends/followers on Facebook at an average growth of 7 friends/followers per day since 2008
> Over 1,500 t-shirts worn, nearly in succession
> Countless media appearances and interviews due to being creative and continuing to push the envelope
> Guest posting for big media outlets' websites (including Entrepreneur.com, *Inc.* magazine, CNBC, and others)

And that doesn't include the incredible amount of content I created (photos, videos, tweets, etc). I spent four years working diligently to build up my online profile so that it looked valuable to a brand that wanted unique exposure. There were countless people who emailed me asking if I could help them sell their last names, but I knew it wouldn't work for them because they hadn't built any type of following or reputation online. Maybe if 100 people all wanted to change their name, a company would be interested in that? I don't know. But that didn't interest me and I couldn't control that.

But this is where you should have hope.

I'm not a celebrity, I'm not a professional athlete, I'm not a billionaire; I'm just a regular guy who decided to do something out of the box. With a bit of unconventional thinking, a lot of hard work, and understanding what value I had to offer, I've created profitable businesses that I can be proud of. I've also created a lifestyle I genuinely love, and I haven't hated a Monday since 2007.

I hope that after reading my story and the practical steps I've shared, it helps spark your next big idea. I strongly believe that every single person has his or hew own unique gift (niche talent) and

On TheBaldFatGuy.com, I share my experiences (via video) with shaving products I have been sent by companies and my fellow bald folk. #shave

can provide huge value through selling a product or service; you just need to put in the work to unleash your creativity. Being an entrepreneur is the hardest, most awesome job you'll ever take on, and I hope these stories have given you a glimpse of what it takes to make money doing what you love.

Good luck, my friends! I can't wait to see what you create!

I don't always twist my words, but when I do I call it TEKST. (Yup, the same TEKST from Chapter 20!) TEKSTartist.com

THE END

503 Motoring is a PNW Custom Automotive Styling Shop that specializes in exemplary customer service. Visit us at 503motoring.com.

ABOUT THE AUTHOR

Jason SurfrApp (formerly Jason Headsetsdotcom & Jason Sadler) is an unconventional marketer and entrepreneur living in Ponte Vedra Beach, FL. He created IWearYourShirt, a company that used sponsored t-shirts to promote businesses on social media, and in 2012 and 2013, he auctioned off his last name to the highest bidders. Jason has been featured by *The Today Show, CBS Evening News, USA Today,* and *The New York Times*.

As a creative entrepreneur, it's Jason's goal to always find a way to make a living doing what he loves, and he's developed a passion for helping others achieve that same thing. Jason can often be found traveling to conferences and events where he speaks to audiences about his unique story and helps them learn to think outside the box. If you're interested in having Jason speak at your next event, contact him via email.

Here are some ways to get in touch with Jason and continue to follow his entrepreneurial journey:

Jason's email list: *therebelwithinus.com*
Personal blog: *jasonsadler.com*
Twitter: *@iwearyourshirt*
Facebook: *facebook.com/jasondoesstuff*
Contact email: *jason@sponsormybook.com*

THANK YOU

I know it's cliché, but there are simply too many people to thank for making this book happen. I do want to take a moment to give special thanks to my Mom and Grama (and of course the rest of my family) for supporting all my crazy entrepreneurial adventures over the years. I know it's been a rocky ride at times, but I can't thank you enough for the guidance and help over the years. I love you guys. To my girlfriend Caroline. You're an incredibly talented lady (you designed the cover of this book, duh) and I'm grateful to have you in my life. Nothing I do could be done without you and I appreciate you more than I tell you. I love you, Carol. Extra special thank you to the entire RTC (Round Table Companies) family for helping me make this a real book. Lizzie, you're just freakin' awesome. I can't thank you enough for working under my insanely tight deadlines and helping pull all the content of this book out of my brain (and then reorganizing it with me many times). Dave, without you and our lunch meeting in early 2013, this book wouldn't exist. I appreciate all your support and willingness to move other RTC projects around to help get my book done. Nothing but love, dude! Seth Fendley, thanks for being so awesome over the years and stepping up to help organize this book. And Shane Mac, you kept me sane during some of my roughest times in 2013 and have been a huge inspiration and mentor to me. You're a great guy and I can't thank you enough for your continued support.

I also want to thank the IWearYourShirt community. Without you, I wouldn't have a book to write. You helped me create and grow a weird idea I had in my closet, to the "thing" that I've built my entrepreneurial life around. I will never forget all the Ustream shows, the chats on Twitter and Facebook, and the support you continue to show for all of my crazy projects. Speaking of IWearYourShirt, I want to thank Evan White, Heather Macdonald, DeAndre Upshaw, Angela Mayans, Amber Plaster, Neal Brooks, Bimini Wright, Sarah Beal, and Burton Hohman for all your hard work and dedication to the company I built. Some of us don't talk anymore and I know I've made mistakes. I hope you realize how much I truly appreciated the time and effort you put into IWearYourShirt. Sean Ely, I bet you thought I forgot about you, huh? You're the red-headed brother I never had. Thank you for moving to Florida and working your ass of for me. I'll never forget the tough times you, Caroline, and I went through together. We miss you and Lionel.

And last but certainly not least, I want to thank the sponsors and supporters of this book. Without you, SponsorMyBook.com would have been a failure and this book would never have been written. It means the world to me that you invested your money into this project and I hope it brings you value.

Oh, one more . . . **Thank you, readers of this book!** Please reach out to me and let me know you read my book and what you thought of it (even if you hated it). I'd love to personally thank each and every one of you (*jason@sponsormybook.com*).

treehouse™

I want to give a shout out to the entire team at Treehouse (especially Ryan and Faye). I couldn't ask for a better company to be the Front Cover sponsor of my book. It's my hope that everyone reading this book goes to *www.jointreehouse.com/jason* and at least signs up for a free trial account. The courses Treehouse offers on design, development, small business, etc, are absolutely amazing. I learned more in two weeks on Treehouse than I did my entire time in college (and that's no exaggeration!). They truly are helping people achieve their dreams and change the world, one vision at a time.

Seriously, sign up for a Treehouse account. Learn the skills to land your dream job, even without a degree. You won't be disappointed!

www.jointreehouse.com/jason
@treehouse (on Twitter)

There is no better company in the world creating a sense of community and love than RTC (Round Table Companies). This book couldn't have happened without RTC grabbing the Back Cover sponsorship. More importantly, I've met some of the greatest human beings alive through them. The Adventure Trip in early 2014 is one I'll never forget, and I've made new friends for life. I absolutely love the amazing content in the RTC Community (*community. roundtablecompanies.com*).

I encourage everyone reading this book to check it out. There's no cost. No account. Only great people sharing great things. Follow my lead and join the RTC family (I promise there's no weird Kool-Aid to drink!).

Also, if you're interested in writing your own book, check out RTC's authoring services and feel free to reach out to David Cohen (*david@roundtablecompanies.com*).

Join the RTC Community *community.roundtablecompanies.com*
@RTcompanies (on Twitter)

To my friend Richard at GoStats: thank you for being one of the first people to sponsor this book. Not only did you sponsor it, but you also grabbed the Front Inside Flap sponsorship before any other cover sponsors were sold. I think I log into GoStats about twice a day, and love how simple and easy GoStats makes it to see all my website analytics. Plus, no other analytics company can compare to you guys on real-time analytics. You keep it simple and do it right.

To the reader, I highly recommend GoStats and have used it on all my websites. It's 100% free to create an account, and is incredibly simple to use. Plus they create some fun 3D graphs with your data. Weeee, 3D graphs!

www.gostats.com

If you've visited the CreativityForSale.com website, you've seen Design Extensions work in action! My girlfriend, Caroline, did the illustrations, but Jay Owen and his team at Design Extensions made the website come to life. I know Jay personally and he's a really great guy. I can't imagine a better company to point you toward if you need design and development work of any kind (including branding, marketing, printing, and more!).

Thanks for taking a chance on this project, Jay, and double thanks for putting the Creativity For Sale website together on super short notice!

www.designextensions.com
facebook.com/designextensions
@designext (on Twitter)

OFFICIAL SPONSORMYBOOK SUPPORTERS

Francis Ablola
Tynishia Abov
Austin Adamson
Aimee Adler
Jason Applebaum
Jan Aubert
Adam Avitable
Brendan Barry
William Bell
Heran Bellu
Veronica Berry
Michael Bertrand
Bud Bilanich
Rodney Blackwell
Katie Boucher
Cindy Brown
Lyla Burston
David Burzynski
Jordan Cable
Colin Capenito
Chad Capp
Bryan Carr
Phillip Censky
Kris Chislett
Kevin Christensen
Catherine Colgan
Nick Collins
Aaron Curtis
Cameron Davison
Nathan Davison
Nelson de Witt
Jeff DeHaven
Frank Dickson
Diane Lamperti Donney
John Downey
Richard Dupon
Ulil Estrada
Seth Fendley
Brent Fine
Ashley Flitter
Brian Gioia
Coty Gonzales

Tony Green
Nick·Grice
The Grice Family
Sonia Gutierrez
Scott Hale
Wade Hammes
Dakota Herrera
Burton Hohman
Austin Holsinger
Ethan Hong
Justin James
Susan James
Tim Jones
Andy Jones
Garrett Kaule
Chad Kelly
Damien Kelly
Jared Kleinert
Casey Koppenhoefer
Chad Kraft
Travis & Kelsey Kroger
Siv Lam
Lisa Lambert
Justin Levy
David Lewis
Ryan Lund
Renee Marshall-McKinley
Tim McAlpine
Jonathan Miller
Bron Mitchell
Scott Mittleman
Grama & Grampa Moorman
April Mraz
Steven Muncie
Kelly Murphy
Luke Mysse
Ashley Nialetz
Ashley Oblad
Brock Picken
Ben Przeslak
Brandi Rathburn
Tom Rauen

Hila Raz
Sue Anne Reed
Scott Rench
Zane Safrit
Jeff Schmitt
Amy Schmittauer
Adam Schomaker
Shannon Scott
Richard Seidel
Courtney Shabram-Beach
Mark Shinn
Jacob Shuttleworth
Narinder Singh
Dawn Skaggs
Rebecca Smith
Benjamin Smithee
Gerardo Sordo Fernández
Nicolo S.
Caron Streibich
Chris Strom
Jordan Sullivan
Oz Sultan
Ken Surritte
Marsh Sutherland
Theresa Thielking
Briana Tinnin
Sofie Todd
Sacha Tueni
Lewis Turner
Paris Turnquist
Dawn Veselka
Jimmy Vinicky
Kate Volman
Chris Vuotto
Daniela Wallroff
Matthew Welzenbach
Kenneth Westling
Bradley Wood
Weston Woodward
Jessica Ziegler
Leah Zorn

You thought it was over right? Just one last thank you for reading! Oh, and word-of-mouth is crucial for any author. I'd really appreciate if you took two minutes to leave a review of Creativity For Sale on Amazon.com. Reviews are very important to authors and even if your review is only a line or two, it would make a huge difference.

Visit *CreativityForSale.com/amazon* to leave a review.

NOW GO OUT INTO THE WORLD AND MAKE

AWESOME

WHERE AWESOME IS NOT!